PROMISED
LAND

Other books by Derek Prince

PROMISED LAND

THE FUTURE OF ISRAEL REVEALED IN PROPHECY

DEREK PRINCE

Chosen

Grand Rapids, Michigan

Published by Chosen Books
A division of Baker Publishing Group
P.O. Box 6287, Grand Rapids, MI 49516-6287
www.chosenbooks.com

Formerly published as *The Last Word on the Middle East*, copyright 1982 by Derek Prince and published by Chosen Books. Updates for this new edition were approved by Derek Prince, with the exception of chronological updates since June 2002, which were made by the editorial staff of Derek Prince Ministries, P.O. Box 19501, Charlotte, NC 28219-9501.

Printed in the United States of America

Library of Congress Cataloging-in-Publication Data
Prince, Derek.
    Promised land : the future of Israel revealed in prophecy / Derek Prince.
        p.   cm.
    Rev. ed. of : The last word on the Middle East. c1982.
    Includes bibliographical references.
    ISBN 0-8007-9389-7 (pbk.)
        1. Jews—Restoration. 2. Bible—Prophecies—Israel. 3. Israel. 4. Jewish-Arab relations. I. Prince, Derek. Last word on the Middle East. II. Title.
BS649.J5P69 2005
231.7'45—dc22   2004018746

CONTENTS

PREFACE

Since the end of World War II, the focus of world politics has shifted from Europe and North America to the Middle East. Today's news media devote more attention to the Middle East than to any other area on earth. Here are centered the issues and conflicts that could, overnight, spark off the next worldwide conflagration—perhaps to be known as World War III.

Two main factors have contributed to this dramatic increase in the importance of the Middle East: *oil* and *Israel*. Almost all the developed nations of the world today are dependent, in varying degrees, upon a continuing supply of oil from sources in the Arab states of the Middle East. Thus oil has become an international political weapon. Through its use, the Arab nations command a measure of influence worldwide that they could never have achieved otherwise.

Even more significant is the emergence of Israel as a sovereign Jewish state. Unceasingly opposed and assailed from its birth until now, this tiny state has consistently confounded the experts and radically changed the political and military balance of the Middle East. Any valid assessment of the overall situation there must first come to grips with the unique role Israel has played and continues to play.

In this book, I offer what I believe to be the key to interpreting the role of Israel and, therefore, the key to a realistic projection of future events in the Middle East. This key was placed in my hand through circumstances not of my own choosing: five years of service during World War II with the British Army in Egypt, Libya, the Sudan and, finally, Palestine. This was followed by two more years of residence in Palestine as a civilian. During these years, I witnessed and participated in the tumultuous events out of which the present situation in the Middle East has emerged.

Since that time, I have maintained ongoing contact with people and events in Israel and the surrounding countries.

Derek Prince
Jerusalem

PART I

Historical Perspective

1

WHERE HISTORY
AND PROPHECY MEET

On a fine night in April 1946, I stood on a saddle of land uniting Mount Scopus on the north with the Mount of Olives on the south. Before me to the west, the gold Dome of the Rock and the silver dome of the Mosque of Al Aksa glistened in the moonlight. Around and behind them, the Old City of Jerusalem, with its serrated walls and towers and its variegated rooftops, seemed to sleep peacefully, awaiting the predawn call of the Muslim muezzin from the mosque.

Yet I knew that the peaceful appearance was deceptive. Beneath the surface lay forces already at work that would inevitably erupt in violence and bloodshed.

Behind me stood the massive stone buildings and the square tower of the Augusta Victoria Hospice. Built originally as a hospice for pilgrims from Europe, it had been taken over by the British authorities in World War II for use as a military hospital. Within its walls, I had completed my service as a hospital attendant and was now ready to be discharged from the Army.

I found myself at a watershed in my life. I had just married Lydia Christensen, a former schoolteacher from Denmark, whom I had met in Jerusalem. Lydia was "mother" to a small children's home located in Ramallah, an Arab town ten miles north of Jerusalem. Through my marriage to her, I had become "father" to the eight girls then in her home, ranging in age from four to eighteen. Of these eight girls, six were Jewish, one was Arab and the youngest was English.

Since Lydia and I planned to go on making our home in Ramallah, I had arranged to take my discharge from the Army in Jerusalem.

"What Lies Ahead?"

As I lingered there on the mountain, savoring the beauty of Jerusalem, I found myself asking, "What lies ahead?" I was thinking not merely of Lydia and myself and our girls, but also of all the people of that land, with their unique intermingling of races, cultures and religions.

The future of the whole area was in the melting pot. Different racial and political groups were advancing claims to both territory and sovereignty that could not be reconciled with each other. The British government had come forward with a series of proposed "solutions" to the apparent impasse. Invariably, however, solutions that were acceptable to one group were rejected outright by the others. Was there any other source from which to seek a solution? I had come to believe that there was.

In the course of nearly six years in the Army, I had become a dedicated student of the Bible. Throughout three weary years in the sandy wastes of North Africa, my Bible had been my constant companion, my unfailing source of comfort and strength. At one point, I had been hospitalized for a full year with a skin condition that did not yield to any medical treatment available in that situation. I had regained my health only when I dared to forgo further medication and trust simply in the Bible's clear promises of physical healing.

In this and many other ways, I had proved to my own satisfaction that the teachings of the Bible, when acted on in faith, are still as valid and vital as when they were first written.

In 1944, however, when the Army transferred me to Palestine, I found myself confronted with Bible truth in a totally new dimension. Up to that time, I had read the Bible as though it had been written in a vacuum. I wholeheartedly embraced the spiritual truths it contained, but they were detached from any context in space or time.

Now I came to see the Bible in a specific geographical setting. I realized that the events recorded in it took place within an area that had its lateral axis in the Mediterranean, with Italy as its western limit and Persia as its eastern limit. By far the greatest part of them took place within a much smaller area about the size of New Jersey, known variously as the land of Canaan, the land of Israel, Palestine or the Holy Land.

In the time of the patriarchs, I learned, this area was known as Canaan. After its conquest by the Israelites under Moses and Joshua, it became the land of Israel. This name is still used in the New Testament (see Matthew 2:20), even though the area was by then a province of the Roman Empire.

The name *Palestine* means "land of the Philistines." It was first used by the Greeks, then by the Romans and other subsequent Gentile rulers, including the British. The title "the Holy Land" has been used by Christians from about the fifth century onward. Following the termination of the British Mandate in 1948 and the subsequent Arab/Israeli conflict, the land was divided between the two states of Israel and Jordan. (Subsequent to the Oslo Peace Accord of 1993, the area has been gradually redefined as Israeli and Palestinian territories.)

When I viewed the events described in the Bible in this geographical context, they became real and vivid for me in an altogether new way. Zechariah, for example, had described the very spot on which I stood in his graphic prophecy of the Lord's return to the earth:

> On that day his feet will stand on the Mount of Olives, east of Jerusalem, and the Mount of Olives will be split in two from east to west, forming a great valley, with half of the mountain moving north and half moving south. . . . On that day living water will flow out from Jerusalem, half to the eastern sea and half to the western sea, in summer and in winter.
>
> Zechariah 14:4, 8

Before me, I could almost visualize the events he described. Our hospital building—the Augusta Victoria Hospice—was situated just where the earthquake was due to take place. About twenty years previously, the building's square tower had been cracked by an earth tremor, which had rendered the tower permanently unsafe to climb. History had confirmed that the area was subject to earthquakes.

To the west, across the Kidron Valley, various geological surveys had discovered indications of underground reservoirs of water beneath the city of Jerusalem. Geologically, the stage was set for the events predicted by Zechariah.

So exactly did the prophet's words fit the scene before me that I could picture the water released by the earthquake welling up from the Temple area and flowing out toward me through the east-west valley that would be created—just about where my feet were then planted.

I recalled a parallel passage in Ezekiel, which likewise pictures water flowing from Jerusalem eastward toward the Dead Sea:

> The man brought me back to the entrance of the temple, and I saw water coming out from under the threshold of the temple toward the east (for the temple faced east). The water was coming down from under the south side of the temple, south of the altar. He then brought me out through the north gate and led me around the outside to the outer gate facing east, and the water was flowing from the south side.
>
> As the man went eastward with a measuring line in his hand, he measured off a thousand cubits and then led me through water that was ankle-deep. He measured off another thousand cubits and led me through water that was knee-deep. He measured off another thousand and led me through water that was up to the waist. He measured off another thousand, but now it was a river that I could not cross, because the water had risen and was deep enough to swim in—a river that no one could cross. . . .
>
> He said to me, "This water flows toward the eastern region and goes down into the Arabah, where it enters the Sea. When it empties into the Sea, the water there becomes fresh. Swarms of living creatures will live wherever the river flows. There will be large numbers

of fish, because this water flows there and makes the salt water fresh; so where the river flows everything will live. . . .
   Fruit trees of all kinds will grow on both banks of the river. Their leaves will not wither, nor will their fruit fail. Every month they will bear, because the water from the sanctuary flows to them. Their fruit will serve for food and their leaves for healing."

Ezekiel 47:1–5, 8–9, 12

With this picture still in mind, I turned and walked a few hundred yards to the eastern slope of the mountain. In the distance, the Dead Sea gleamed in the moonlight like a jewel set in the folds of the hills. The high chemical content of its waters gave them a unique luster. In the foreground, the barren, bony ridges of the Judean hills descended to the area Ezekiel called the "Arabah." Beyond doubt, this area needed the miracle-working transformation provided by the living waters that Ezekiel saw in his vision!

While living there on the Mount of Olives, I had learned that *Arabah* is the Hebrew name for the Jordan Valley, as it extends from the place where the Jordan River enters the Dead Sea southward to the Gulf of Aqaba. From the Temple Mount on the west to the Dead Sea and the Arabah on the east, every detail in the descriptions of both Zechariah and Ezekiel was exact and vivid. The descriptions fit perfectly with the entire terrain. Detached from this geographical context, however, they were meaningless.

The same principle, I realized, would apply to countless other Bible passages, both historical and prophetic.

A People and Their History

Later that night, as I lay in bed, my mind was still busy with the impressions of the past two years. At the same time I had been introduced to the land of the Bible, I had also been introduced to the people whose history is the Bible's central theme. I had come to see that geography and history are in fact interwoven.

Geographically, the Bible is set in the land of Israel; historically, its theme is the people of Israel. I marveled that, in all my Bible reading, I had overlooked a fact so simple and so obvious. Yet once I grasped this fact, it gave a new clarity and cohesiveness to the whole Bible.

The first eleven chapters of the Bible, I realized, serve as an introduction. They fill in the background and set the stage for all that is to follow. From then on, the Bible is essentially the history of Abraham and the nation descended from him through Isaac and Jacob—that is to say, Israel.

There was, I discovered, a distinction to be made between the words *Israel* and *Israelite* and the words *Jew* and *Jewish*. Linguistically, *Jew* is derived directly from *Judah*, the name of one of the twelve tribes of Israel. From the time of the Babylonian captivity, however, all the Israelites who returned to the land of Israel were called Jews, irrespective of their tribal background. This usage is carried over into the New Testament. Paul, for example, was from the tribe of Benjamin; yet he called himself a Jew (see Acts 21:39).

In contemporary usage, these four words are not fully interchangeable. *Israel* and *Israelite* focus primarily on national origin and background. *Jew* and *Jewish* focus more on religion, culture and later history. Since the birth of the state of Israel in 1948, the word *Israeli* has been added, referring to any citizen of the state, whether of Jewish, Arab or Druse descent.

One unique feature of the history of Israel, as recorded in the Bible, is that part of it was written after the events, as normal history is, while the remainder was written in advance of the events, as prophecy. Taken together, the historical and prophetic portions of the Bible constitute a complete history of the people of Israel.

Though large sections of this history are given only in outline, other sections contain vivid and detailed descriptions. The prophetic writings are most intriguing, since in many cases they were written centuries before the events they describe. Yet they still combine a degree of accuracy and vividness that could not have been excelled by an eyewitness.

My evaluation of the Bible as essentially a history of Israel, embracing both the past and the future, did not altogether surprise me, so long as I applied it only to the Old Testament. But as a Christian, I came to the New Testament from the unconscious perspective of centuries of Christian tradition. It was hard to evaluate the facts objectively.

It seemed logical to begin with the identity of Jesus Himself. Without any question, He is the one supremely important person in the New Testament. Apart from Him, indeed, the New Testament would never have been written. It is equally beyond question that during His earthly life, Jesus was, by every possible standard, an Israelite.

The New Testament makes it clear, however, that the identity of Jesus as an Israelite did not cease with the end of His earthly life. In Revelation 5:5—a passage written more than fifty years after His death and resurrection—Jesus is still described in heaven as "the Lion of the tribe of Judah, the Root of David."

This does not refer to some temporary feature of His brief 33 years on earth. This is His identity after His death and resurrection, throughout all eternity. He is forever "the Lion of the tribe of Judah, the Root of David." He is forever identified with the family of David, the tribe of Judah, the people of Israel. He is forever an Israelite.

Next, I turned my attention to the character and contents of the four gospels. These constitute the historical basis for all the fundamental tenets of the Christian faith (as they are stated, for example, in the great creeds of the Church).

Once again, the facts spoke for themselves. Except for a brief visit to Egypt by Joseph and Mary and the infant Jesus, *all* the events described in *all* the gospels took place within the borders of the land of Israel.

Furthermore, well over 90 percent of the people portrayed in the gospels are Israelites. The only exceptions are a tiny handful of non-Jewish persons, such as the Magi from the east and the Samaritan woman at Jacob's well, as well as a sprinkling of Roman officials and military personnel. Essentially, the gospels are a record of Israelites, set in the land of Israel.

Next, I considered the authorship of the New Testament. The picture that emerged was no different. Every one of its 27 books was authored by an Israelite. A question could be raised concerning Luke, the author of the gospel named after him and also of the book of Acts, since it is generally accepted that Luke was of Gentile origin. But because he was a proselyte to Judaism, he, too, became identified with Israel.

It is true, of course, that after the Day of Pentecost, the message of the Gospel was rapidly spread abroad throughout the civilized world. Multitudes of Gentiles acknowledged Jesus as their Savior and were added to the Church.

When I began to ask, however, who the main human instruments, recorded as spreading the Gospel and establishing churches, were in the New Testament, I had to acknowledge that almost without exception they were Jewish. All the twelve apostles were Jewish. Paul, who became the great apostle of the Gentiles, was likewise Jewish. Most of Paul's co-workers, such as Barnabas and Silas, were Jewish. Even Timothy, by virtue of his Jewish mother, was legally reckoned to be Jewish and, therefore, needed to be circumcised (see Acts 16:1–3).

I tried to think of a Gentile Christian who played a major role in the New Testament record. At first no name came to me. Eventually, I decided that Titus may have had the best claim. He was a trusted co-worker of Paul, and at least a book of the New Testament was named after him. No one could claim, however, that Titus was one of the major figures of the New Testament.

It remained for me to consider the prophetic sections of the New Testament. Was their emphasis in some way different from that of the historical sections? What kind of picture of the future did they paint? So far as I could see, their emphasis on the unique role of Israel is in no way diminished.

The writer of Hebrews tells us that the ultimate goal of all true believers is "the city with foundations, whose architect and builder is God" (Hebrews 11:10). In Revelation 21, this city is described for us. On its gates are inscribed the names of the twelve tribes of Israel. On its foundations are the names of the twelve apostles of Jesus. Every name inscribed in the new Jerusalem is an Israelite name.

In summary, then, we may state the following:

- All 39 books of the Old Testament were written by Jewish authors.

- Jesus was born a Jew, died a Jew and will return as a Jew.
- All the events of the gospels (except the flight to Egypt) took place in Israel.
- Over 90 percent of the people portrayed in the gospels are Israelites.
- Every one of the 27 books of the New Testament has Jewish authorship. (Luke might be regarded as a possible exception, but he was a proselyte to Judaism.)
- The main instruments for establishing churches and spreading the gospel were Jewish.
- All twelve apostles were Jewish.
- The future city in Revelation is inscribed with the names of the twelve tribes of Israel.
- The city's foundations carry the names of the twelve apostles of Jesus.

Surely, I reflected, no one with anti-Semitic prejudice could ever feel comfortable there!

Combining my survey of the New Testament with that of the Old, I came to a clear and simple conclusion: The Bible is essentially a record of Israel written by Israelites, partly in the form of history and partly in the form of prophecy.

Exile—and Return

Why, then, did it seem strange—in fact, almost unthinkable—to associate the Jewish people with the New Testament? As I pondered this question, I saw that toward the end of the first century, there had been a very significant break in the continuum of history. Moreover, this break had been passed over in almost total silence by the versions of history I had studied in Britain.

There were two aspects to this break: First, the people of Israel had been separated from their land. Second, at just about the same time, they had been separated from their role as leaders in disseminating the Gospel and building the Church.

This double break determined their role in history for the next eighteen centuries. They had become a nation of exiles. Physically, they were exiled from the only land where they had ever known nationhood. Spiritually, they were exiled from the very religion of which they themselves were the founders.

Over the past two years, I had witnessed part of the process of healing the first of these two breaks—that between the people of Israel and their land. Did the logic of history indicate that this would be a prelude to the healing of the second break—that between the people of Israel and the Christian Church?

Many people, I knew, would dismiss this suggestion as inconceivable. And yet, a century earlier, just as many people would have dismissed as inconceivable the suggestion that the people of Israel would ever be restored to their land. I was living in the midst of a land and a people whose entire history was full of events that would have been dismissed by most people as inconceivable.

As I searched for a way to express the significance of the events I had been witnessing, I formed a mental picture of an old grandfather clock. For many years, I imagined, it had stood in the corner of an antique store. The hands never moved; no sound came from it. Everyone assumed that the mechanism was out of order. Then one day, without a human hand touching it, the clock began again to tick, and the hands began to move. Now the clock was no longer just an interesting relic from the past. Once again, it was telling the time.

Israel was God's prophetic clock. By restoring the people to the land, God had set the clock once again in motion. After long centuries of silence, it was now telling the time. If I was interpreting the message of its hands rightly, they were marking off the closing hours of an age of history that had lasted something like nineteen centuries.

Survivors of the Holocaust

My introduction to the people of Israel coincided with one of the most tragic and critical periods in their long and often tragic history.

The unutterable horror of the Holocaust was just beginning to make its full impact upon the Jewish community around the world, but nowhere to a greater degree than in the land of Israel.

In spite of a blockade imposed by the British Army and Navy, a trickle of Jewish survivors from Europe was making its way by various routes to Palestine. I found myself, almost against my will, listening to accounts of suffering and cruelty that I had never believed possible. From time to time, I witnessed the reunion of family members who had been separated from each other in Europe but who had somehow survived and escaped, to meet again in Israel.

My exposure to Israel's geography had already given a new direction to my study of the Bible. Now my firsthand exposure to this aspect of Israel's history was even more revolutionary in its impact upon me. I began to discover countless passages in almost all the Old Testament prophets predicting that, before the present age comes to its close, there is to be a great ingathering of Jewish people from all over the world to the land of Israel. Nor were these predictions confined to the Old Testament. I discovered corresponding passages in the teaching of Jesus in the New Testament, which indicate that the closing drama of the present age will be enacted in the land of Israel.

Up to this time, I had viewed such passages as vague, almost Utopian pictures that somehow inspired hope of a better age to come. Now, however, I saw that they were precise, specific predictions that were being fulfilled before my eyes. In many of these predictions, certain salient features were singled out for mention, just as if the writer had himself been an eyewitness.

I found many examples of this in the prophet Jeremiah. One passage became particularly vivid for me:

"Return, faithless people," declares the LORD, "for I am your husband. I will choose you—one from a town and two from a clan —and bring you to Zion. . . . In those days the house of Judah will join the house of Israel, and together they will come from a northern land to the land I gave your forefathers as an inheritance."

Jeremiah 3:14, 18

This passage emphasizes the return of the Israelites from "a northern land" to the land God had given to their forefathers. Indisputably, the latter is the land of Israel. "A northern land" would include Russia, Poland, Germany and other countries in Eastern Europe and the Balkans. In 1946, that was precisely the area from which the majority of Jewish refugees were making their way to Israel.

What particularly impressed me was the detail "one from a town and two from a clan." This corresponded exactly with what I was hearing from Jewish people around me. Many times a survivor's story would go like this: "I'm the only one in our family from Berlin who has survived. But I've met just one other member of the family who has also survived—my uncle from Hannover."

In each story, the name of the town might differ. The country might be Poland or Austria rather than Germany. Rather than an uncle, it might be a married sister, or a cousin or a nephew. But the essential feature of Jeremiah's prophecy remained the same: "One from a town and two from a clan."

In most cases, I felt sure, these Jewish people had no idea they were quoting the words of one of their own prophets, who predicted—2,500 years beforehand—the very events they had lived through.

God Watches Over His Word

I began to see history in a new light—not as the random interplay of unpredictable forces, whether political or military or economic, but as the outworking of divine purposes unfolded in advance through the prophetic Word of God. Nowhere was this principle illustrated more clearly than in the call of Jeremiah to the prophetic ministry, as he himself recounts it:

> The word of the LORD came to me, saying,
>
> "Before I formed you in the womb I knew you,
>   before you were born I set you apart;
>   I appointed you as a prophet to the nations."

"Ah, Sovereign LORD," I said, "I do not know how to speak; I am only a child."

But the LORD said to me, "Do not say, 'I am only a child.' You must go to everyone I send you to and say whatever I command you. Do not be afraid of them, for I am with you and will rescue you," declares the LORD.

Then the LORD reached out his hand and touched my mouth and said to me, "Now, I have put my words in your mouth. See, today I appoint you over nations and kingdoms to uproot and tear down, to destroy and overthrow, to build and to plant."

Jeremiah 1:4–10

There is a remarkable paradox implicit in this account. On the one hand, a position of tremendous authority is promised to Jeremiah, "over nations and kingdoms to uproot and tear down, to destroy and overthrow, to build and to plant."

On the other hand, Jeremiah considered himself to be "only a child." Furthermore, there was little outward evidence in his subsequent career of this authority God had promised him. He was rejected consistently by most of his own people; frequently misrepresented and mishandled; confined for a while in a dungeon; almost allowed to die in a well shaft.

Wherein, then, lay Jeremiah's authority, and how was it exercised? I concluded that the answer was to be found in the act by which God set Jeremiah in his prophetic office: "Then the LORD reached out his hand and touched my mouth and said to me, 'Now, I have put my words in your mouth.'"

The authority was not in Jeremiah as a person; it was in God's words put into Jeremiah's mouth. These words, as he spoke them forth, determined the destinies of all the nations and kingdoms concerning which he prophesied. Rulers and peoples would reject Jeremiah as a person, but they could not annul the prophetic words he spoke concerning them. When Jeremiah died, the prophetic words he had spoken lived on, shaping the ongoing destinies of those peoples.

Though later generations either forgot or ignored Jeremiah's words, God did neither. For He had assured Jeremiah, "I am watching to see that my word is fulfilled" (verse 12). The words of God through Jeremiah centered primarily on his own people, Israel, but they also extended to a much wider circle. Jeremiah, as a "prophet to the nations," predicted the destinies of many other countries beside Israel, including all the nations that make up the area we know today as the Middle East.

Furthermore, God not only assured Jeremiah that He would watch over Jeremiah's words to see that they were fulfilled; He also made specific provision that Jeremiah's words would be preserved until the time came for their final outworking:

> "This is what the LORD, the God of Israel, says: 'Write in a book all the words I have spoken to you. The days are coming,' declares the LORD, 'when I will bring my people Israel and Judah back from captivity and restore them to the land I gave their forefathers to possess,' says the LORD."
>
> Jeremiah 30:2–3

Clearly God was looking forward through the centuries to the time when He would regather Israel in the land He had appointed for them. He foresaw that, at that time, His people would enter into a fuller understanding of all that had been predicted for them in the words of Jeremiah.

With a sense of awe and excitement, I realized that I had been privileged to become an eyewitness of the events Jeremiah had predicted.

Here, then, was the answer to the question I had been asking myself earlier that evening: What lies ahead? The Word of God, spoken many centuries previously through His prophets, was still shaping the ongoing destinies not only of Israel, but also of the other nations round about. His Word provided the only reliable key to interpreting the situation that was developing in the Middle East.

Before I finally fell asleep, however, I concluded that I was not yet ready to apply this key to the present and the future. First, I needed a clearer understanding of the past. With this, I would be better able to interpret the new factors in world history that had precipitated the radical changes now taking place in the Middle East.

2

THE DREAM THAT
CAME TO PASS

My experiences in Palestine had given me a new perspective of the previous nineteen centuries. I realized that I had been brought face-to-face with a major stream of history with which, up to that time, I had been completely unfamiliar. My own main field of study had been the classics, covering the history of Greek and Roman civilization from the time of Homer to the breakup of the Roman Empire.

I had also been required to familiarize myself with the general course of European history, with particular emphasis on that of my own country, Britain. My knowledge of Jewish history had ended more or less where the New Testament closed. From this perspective, the war between the Jews and Rome, ending with the destruction of Jerusalem in AD 70, was presented as a minor incident of Roman history. From then on, it was as though the Jewish people had ceased to have any significant history.

Now I began to understand that Jewish history was something like a river whose course had been affected by an earthquake. The greater part of its water had descended into a chasm created by the earthquake, where it continued to flow. Because its new course was mostly underground, many people assumed that the river had ceased to flow altogether. Even those who knew that the river was still flowing were not aware of the exact course it was following.

Toward the end of the nineteenth century, however, the river of Jewish history emerged once more into the open landscape of world history, producing a powerful impact on culture, science and politics. Though the river first reemerged as a seemingly insignificant trickle, it gained steadily in volume, until its impact was now being felt throughout the Middle East.

The most distinctive (and ultimately the most significant) form in which Jewish history found new expression was Zionism: the belief in the reestablishment of an independent Jewish state in the Jews' historic homeland.

How did a crushed nation "survive" for all those centuries? What events could possibly have thrust the goals of Zionism into the forefront of world affairs?

Ever since the destruction of Jerusalem in AD 70, the Jewish people had held to the dream of returning to "Zion." For most, it was little more than a dream. Dispersed throughout the civilized world, sold into slavery, impoverished, persecuted—still they clung to their identity as a people, to their book of the Law (the *Torah*), to the writings of the rabbis, to the observance of the Sabbath and to their traditions. Year after year in the Passover ceremony, they faithfully recited, "Next year in Jerusalem!" But few ever really believed it.

Victims of Theology

Throughout the long centuries of their dispersion, the worst sufferings of the Jewish people were inflicted upon them by Christians. Christian anti-Semitism was based on and nourished by a combination of theology and popular legends.

A succession of prominent Christian theologians taught that the Jews were solely responsible for the death of Christ and were, therefore, guilty of the most terrible of all crimes: "deicide," the murder of God. Being thus under the perpetual and irrevocable curse of God, the Jews deserved, in this view, continual execration and persecution.

Popular legends that persisted into the twentieth century charged the Jews repeatedly with the ritual murder of Christian children, in order to use their blood for secret ceremonies connected with the Passover. Such charges tended to produce two results: the wholesale massacre of Jewish communities and the canonization by the Church of the children purported to have been murdered.

The Christian theologian Lovsky lists ways in which Christian anti-Semitism habitually found expression: contempt, calumnies, animosity, segregation, forced baptisms, appropriation of children, unjust trials, pogroms, exiles, systematic persecutions, thefts, plunder, hatred (open or concealed) and social degradation.[1]

Even in the best of Western literature, the Jews were represented consistently as being rapacious, treacherous, covetous people whose only profession was usury. Shylock, in Shakespeare's *Merchant of Venice*, projects such a stereotype. It is significant that Jews had been banished from England for nearly three hundred years before Shakespeare's day. Thus, his portrait of Shylock was entirely a construction of his own imagination and of popular legend.

It is outside the scope of this book to analyze in detail the reasons for and results of Christian anti-Semitism. For those who desire a balanced, scholarly presentation of this theme, I recommend the book *The Anguish of the Jews*, by Edward H. Flannery. The author is honest and impartial in his exposure of Christian guilt, although he is not anti-Christian. In fact, he is a Catholic priest, committed to both Christianity and the Church.

Dreams—and Dreamers

In this atmosphere of contempt and persecution, the Jews lived as aliens and outcasts from society, a downtrodden people without a country. In their darkness, there was just one ray of light—Zion. Yet this evoked memories of the past more frequently than it did hopes for the future. From time to time, however, a leader would arise to give them a glimmer of hope that they would again be a nation in their own homeland.

One such leader was David Reubeni, a charismatic Jewish figure from the East who appeared in western Europe about the year 1525. Boldly he sought to raise an army to reconquer Palestine for his people. Announcing that his brother was the ruler of a Jewish kingdom near Arabia, Reubeni presented himself first to the Pope.

He reminded the Pope that many earlier Church fathers had believed that Jerusalem would be rebuilt prior to the millennial age. Amazingly, the Pope received him, endorsed him and sent him off with letters of recommendation to the king of Portugal.

The Jewish people rallied to David Reubeni, since he was the first Jewish leader in many centuries of sufficient stature to speak to a Pope and to kings on their behalf. When Reubeni finally reached Charles V, who was emperor of the Holy Roman Empire, however, he was first spurned, then arrested, then probably executed.

Their hopes dashed by this failure, the Jews settled back into their resignation. At the end of the fifteenth century, the Inquisition in Spain and Portugal seemed to seal their fate. Jews were forced to convert or die. In many cases, if the church was not satisfied that their conversion was genuine, they died anyway.

With each new wave of persecution, a few Jews managed to straggle back to Palestine. Some eked out a meager existence on the soil. Others depended on alms sent to them by their more affluent brethren in Europe and Asia. The Crusades of the eleventh and twelfth centuries had left the land desolate and its few inhabitants weak and dispirited. The glories of Jerusalem had long been forgotten.

By the end of the fifteenth century, according to one pilgrim, only four thousand families lived in Jerusalem. Of these, only seventy families were Jewish, and they "of the poorest class, lacking even the commonest necessities."[2] Such a description did not build hope in the hearts of the Jews of Europe for a restored homeland. As Grayzel says further, "The actual state of Palestine had somehow come to stand for the miserable state of the Jewish people. Both were desolate; both were in hostile hands; both awaited God's redemption."[3]

Later, in the sixteenth century, the Jews again experienced a brief moment of hope. Joseph Nasi, a wealthy Portuguese Jew who had fled to Turkey, rose high in the favor of the Sultan. This powerful ruler made Nasi Duke of Naxos, an island in the Aegean Sea, and granted him complete rights to the Tiberias section of Palestine. Nasi planned to use his great wealth and influence to settle a large number of fellow Jews in the area and to obtain silkworms as a means of livelihood for the colony.

Before the plan could be carried out, however, war broke out between Turkey and Venice. In the turmoil, Joseph Nasi fell from favor and lost his power. Again, Jewish hopes were dashed.

Help from an Unexpected Source

At this juncture, when Jewish faith and strength were at their lowest ebb, hope and help came from an unexpected source—Christians in England. The Christian Church there had been as guilty in its attitude and conduct toward the Jews as had the rest of the Church. From 1290, when England deported every Jew living there, the nation had been without a Jewish community.

The translation of the Bible into English in the 1500s, however, heralded a renewed confidence in the authority of Scripture and its relevance to the life of God's people. There also came a spiritual awakening among Christian scholars and laymen alike, which included a new understanding of God's purpose for the Jewish people and for their historic homeland.

The first Christian effort to expound the theory of a regathered Israel cost the author his life. Burned as a heretic in 1589 was Francis Kett, a fellow of Corpus Christi College at my own alma mater, Cambridge.

The idea did not die with him, however, as other Elizabethan churchmen, including the Puritans, began to speak and write about "the calling of the Jews." Almost without exception, those who supported this new interpretation of Bible prophecy assumed that mass voluntary conversion to Christianity would precede the Jews' return to their land.

Sir Henry Finch's book, *The Restauration of the Jews*, published in 1621, depicted a perfect theocracy in the restored land of Israel. His prediction—that "all the gentiles shall bring their glory into thy empire"—provoked immediate, violent opposition in both Church and state. King James I considered the book personal libel and arrested the elderly Sir Henry and his publishers. They were held only a few weeks, but the experience caused others to use more discretion in their statements and writings. Still, despite opposition and persecution, the idea had taken root and would continue to grow among the Puritans and others.

The Christian dream of a restored Jewish state flourished in England between 1640 and 1666. It was believed, as David Reubeni proclaimed earlier, that this state would usher in the Messianic age and the Millennium. There was a flurry of ideas, movements and books among men of considerable stature. Oliver Cromwell, Samuel Pepys, Henry Oldenburg, Baruch Spinoza and others—all espoused the doctrine of "Restoration."

In fact, the word itself, when capitalized, came to have that one meaning: the Restoration of Israel. Attention was focused on the Jewish people. Some believed that the Indians of the New World were the "Ten Lost Tribes." Others believed that they themselves were members of the Ten Lost Tribes—persons such as Thomas Tany, a London goldsmith who wanted to bring the Restoration into being. Those who believed this doctrine of "British Israel" were later called "invisible Hebrews." But even as British support grew, persecution of Jews was beginning again in eastern Europe, this time by the Cossacks.

It is not surprising that Sabbatai Zevi, the son of a Jewish tradesman in Smyrna, gained widespread attention in England when he proclaimed himself messiah of the Jewish people. Zevi announced that, in the year 1666, he would lead his people back to their homeland. Fictitious reports that shiploads of Jews were bound for Palestine stirred up as much excitement among non-Jews in London as among the large Jewish population in other cities of Europe. The millenarians were predicting that 1666 would be "the wonderful year."

Sabbatai Zevi did arrive in Constantinople in 1666. But instead of taking the sultan's crown, he became the prisoner of the sultan—and converted to Islam. This time it was not only the hopes of Jews that were dashed. Christians who believed in Restoration felt an almost equal despair.

Writings on This Theme

Two significant writings of this period dropped from sight and did not reappear until the next great wave of Zionism at the end of the nineteenth century. Both these books were written by Christians who studied the biblical prophecies, then looked with the eye of faith across the centuries to a restored nation of Israel.

The first book, *Nova Solyma* (*The Ideal City; Jerusalem Regained*), was a Utopian novel, originally published anonymously in 1648 in Latin. It came to light again only in 1902, the same year in which Theodor Herzl published his novel on the same theme, *Altneuland* (Old New Land).

Nova Solyma was the work of Samuel Gott, who was influenced by John Milton. This book, unlike other Utopian works, is notable because its setting was neither a "Nowhere" nor a "Somewhere," but specifically the land of Israel. The success of the society it portrayed was based on a religion that synthesized Judaism and Christianity.

One striking example of the prophetic insight in this book is the statement put into the mouth of one of its main characters:

> It is fitting in every true republic that we take special care of the young, and in this the providence of God has not made our endeavors ineffectual, for it is well-known that a more beautiful and talented progeny has grown up among us since our restoration.[4]

This description could be applied, without modification, to contemporary Israel.

The other book, *The Way of Light*, by Johann Amos Comenius (Komensky), foresaw a Messianic age that would be preceded by the Restoration of the Jews in their land. Comenius, a Czech pioneer educator living in England, had written his book in 1642, but it was not published until 1667 and then only in Latin. When the book was finally translated into English and printed in 1938, it was obvious that Comenius's thinking was three centuries ahead of his time.

Christian-Jewish Interchange

The most significant Jewish leader in the 1600s was Manasseh ben Israel, rabbi of Amsterdam. His book, *The Hope of Israel*, linked the messianism of the British Puritans with Jewish messianism. He also believed that the Restoration of Israel must include the "Ten Lost Tribes," and he quickly accepted the Puritan notion that the Indians of the New World were these lost kinsmen.

His studies in the book of Daniel, coupled with the prophecy of scattering "from the one end of the earth even unto the other" (Deuteronomy 28:64, KJV), convinced him that England must re-admit Jews within her borders. He worked together with British Christian Restorationists to bring this about, but he did not live to see it happen in the mid-1650s. All the same, his work encouraged those British Christians who were looking for Jewish leaders to bring their vision to pass.

One of the paradoxes of the seventeenth and eighteenth centuries was that many influential Jews did not believe they would be restored to their homeland, while many influential Christians did. A lively debate was sparked in 1787 when Joseph Priestley, a world-renowned naturalist, philosopher and theologian, proposed that Jews acknowledge Jesus as Messiah, come to the end of their sufferings and be gathered to the Holy Land. David Levi, the first Jew to translate the Pentateuch into English, responded with revulsion to Priestley's thesis, especially the idea that the Messiah had already come. His writings demonstrate that most devout Jews of his day were not anticipating either the coming of the Messiah or a return to their land.

The most striking paradox, which endured until the nineteenth century, was that many eminent British thinkers, authors and poets believed strongly in the Restoration movement, while it remained virtually unknown to political leaders.[5]

In 1799, for example, when Napoleon Bonaparte's forces invaded Palestine, leaders of the British Restoration movement called on him to grant the Jews a homeland. These leaders believed that the fall of the Ottoman Empire was inevitable, yet the British government worked tirelessly to preserve Turkey and its dominion. Napoleon's victory was short-lived, however, and his retreat after only one month ended the hope of the Restorationists.

God's plan for the Jews and their homeland took on new importance at this time. In 1800, James Bicheno, in his book *The Restoration of the Jews—Crisis for All Nations*, concluded that Restoration was not conditional on conversion to Christianity. Twenty years later, an anonymous English writer sounded the first call for Christians and Jews to cooperate peacefully to bring a Jewish state into being.

The names of nineteenth-century Christians who embraced the concept of a restored Jewish state read like a section of Who's Who: Charles Darwin, the Earl of Shaftesbury, Lord Palmerstone, Benjamin Disraeli, Robert Browning, George Eliot, John Adams and others.

One of the most colorful supporters was Sir Laurence Oliphant—soldier, diplomat, author, scholar of Russian language and culture, journalist and member of the British Parliament. In about 1878, Oliphant became aware of the plight of European Jewry and set out with characteristic zeal to secure for them "the land of Gilead," east of the Jordan River.

He obtained the endorsement of Lord Salisbury and also of Benjamin Disraeli (Lord Beaconsfield), who was a Jew by birth, a Christian by faith. (Disraeli is considered one of the greatest statesmen the Jewish people have ever produced, and he rose to the highest pinnacle of Western politics of his day—prime minister of the British Empire.) Even the prince of Wales—the future Edward VII—encouraged Oliphant, who then crossed the Channel to Paris to secure the additional support of the French foreign minister.

Armed with documents from the governments of England and France, Oliphant set off for Constantinople to see the sultan. In 1880, at what seemed the most propitious moment for the success of Oliphant's plan, Disraeli fell from power, and the foreign policy of Britain was reversed. No longer would she be the sultan's protector. Again the hopes of British Restorationists, as well as the Jews of Europe, had come to nothing.

Meanwhile, Jewish intellectuals in Russia initiated their own form of Zionism: *Hovevei Zion* ("Lovers of Zion"). They realized that assimilation would not save them from the pogroms (organized massacres) that were the expression of the anti-Semitism then sweeping across Europe. The organization spread rapidly through the Jewish communities on the Continent and to Britain.

Laurence Oliphant joined forces with the Lovers of Zion and worked the rest of his life to help them. As Russian Jews in small numbers began making their way to Palestine, Oliphant and his wife left the comforts of England to settle in Haifa and be on the scene to assist the new arrivals. He died there in 1888, having lived to see new agricultural settlements begun by these refugees from persecution.

Theodor Herzl—and His Friend

The name of Theodor Herzl is forever inscribed in history as the father of modern Zionism. When he came onto the scene, events began to move with remarkable speed. After the first World Zionist Congress in Basel, Switzerland, in 1897, he said, "At Basel I founded the Jewish State! If I said this out loud today I would be greeted by universal laughter. In five years, perhaps, and certainly in fifty years, everyone will perceive it."[6]

Seven years later, Theodor Herzl was dead; but exactly fifty years later, on November 29, 1947, the United Nations voted to establish a Jewish state in Palestine.

Behind these historic scenes was an unknown but most remarkable Christian minister, the chaplain of the British Embassy in Vienna. William Hechler, an Anglican clergyman and son of a Hebrew scholar, became convinced from his study of Bible prophecy that 1897 was the crucial year for the restoration of the Jewish state. Therefore, when he read Herzl's book, *Der Judenstaat* (The Jewish State), three weeks after its publication in 1896, he went directly to Herzl and put himself at Herzl's disposal to help to bring the vision to reality.

Hechler, although an unprepossessing man, had impressive connections. Early in his career, he had served as tutor to the children of Frederic, Grand Duke of Baden, who was the uncle of Kaiser Wilhelm. Furthermore, he had persuaded the grand duke and other members of the German royal family that the Jewish state would be restored, and he had shown them his biblical charts and diagrams. He now offered to open doors for Herzl.

Herzl was not a religious man. He knew little about the prophets. But he was a pragmatist. He recognized that he needed the endorsement and support of secular rulers if he was to gain the respect and support of his Jewish brethren. Furthermore, Hechler was British, and Herzl knew that British Christian Restorationists were probably the strongest allies he could find for his cause. So he accepted Hechler's offer. Within one month of that first encounter, Hechler had arranged a two-hour audience for Herzl with Grand Duke Frederic and had himself spoken directly to Kaiser Wilhelm on Herzl's behalf. Frederic endorsed Herzl's plan and used his influence to arrange meetings with the kaiser, which eventually took place in Constantinople and Jerusalem in October 1898.

It was the audience with Frederic of Baden, however, that made Herzl's name known in the royal courts of Europe and Hechler's tireless efforts—and prayers—that opened other doors for him as well. Herzl's earliest Jewish followers were poor and lacking in influence, but he grew in stature through being received by ministers and even some crowned heads, and the Jewish world began to be encouraged. At last one of their own was speaking on their behalf, claiming their right to independence and their historic homeland!

With William Hechler and British Restorationists on the one side, and Theodor Herzl and the World Zionist Congress on the other, the confluence of the two Zionist streams began. In 1900, the World Zionist Congress met in London, and "Palestine for the Jews" became the rallying cry there.

In 1902, a new wave of pogroms in Russia threw panic into the budding Zionist movement. The World Zionist Congresses in 1902 and 1903 were willing to accept any piece of land anywhere to save the lives of those being mercilessly slaughtered. The British offered land in the Sinai in 1902. When that plan collapsed, the congress of 1903 considered Uganda.

The British Foreign Office officially recognized the Zionist movement as a diplomatic entity in 1903 by its letter offering Uganda as a place of refuge for Jews. Herzl and many others were willing to accept this land in east Africa where they were promised autonomy and self-government, but the congress could not reach agreement. Hechler, an unofficial participant, was one of those who argued that accepting Uganda would save some lives, but it might forever preclude resettlement in their own true homeland.

By August 1904, Herzl was dead. When the congress met again, it abandoned the Uganda plan.

Palestine—the Crucible

Jews continued to stream toward Palestine, meanwhile, like birds in migration. Return to Zion was a dream whose time had come. No longer needing prodding from Christians, they came from Russia and eastern Europe, from Morocco, Iraq, Turkey and Yemen. Between 1904 and 1915, 40,000 immigrants arrived, nearly doubling the Jewish population—still only twelve percent of the total. This was the beginning of the *kibbutz* movement of collective settlements, of the citrus industry, of new towns (such as Tel Aviv in 1909), of social programs and of Jewish industry.

From 1880, when Britain's attitude toward the Ottoman Empire had changed, Germany had been the sultan's protector. The defeat of Germany in World War I, however, changed that situation. When British forces under General Allenby captured Jerusalem from the Turks in 1917, Ottoman rule ended, and British mandatory rule began. General Allenby, a Christian, dismounted from his horse and entered Jerusalem on foot, because "no one but the Messiah should enter this city mounted."

One month earlier, on November 2, 1917, Lord Balfour, the British foreign secretary, had issued a declaration stating, "His Majesty's government views with favour the establishment in Palestine of a national home for the Jewish people." The Balfour Declaration did not create a Jewish state, but it prepared the way for one. Lord Balfour was a Christian who believed in the Restoration of Israel. His declaration caused Christian Restorationists and Jewish Zionists to rejoice together.

This rejoicing was short-lived, however, since no great changes occurred immediately. Until 1920, Palestine was administered by the British military government, which ignored the Balfour Declaration. When the British government eventually appointed their first high commissioner, they chose Herbert Samuel, a Jew, who worked to improve conditions for the new settlers. He also established Hebrew as the third language of the country.

Almost from the outset, there were problems between Arabs and Jews. Various factors contributed to the tension: The policy and methods of the British government differed decisively from those of the Turks who had ruled the area for four hundred years. There was a large influx of Jewish immigrants with heterogeneous backgrounds, cultures and languages. The whole character of the country was undergoing radical change. The Arabs, who strongly resented all this, began to organize anti-Jewish riots.

In 1919, the Zionists had reached amicable agreement with Emir Faisal, the leader of the Arab movement, and believed that they could live peaceably side by side. When Faisal's brother Abdullah moved into eastern Palestine with a band of guerrillas in 1921, however, the situation changed.

Winston Churchill, British secretary of the colonies, recognized Abdullah as emir and, with a stroke of his pen, partitioned Palestine, creating the new mandatory territory of Transjordan. He hoped he would thus placate the Arabs by giving them four-fifths of the total territory. In 1922, the British brought the Palestine question before the League of Nations, which confirmed these boundaries.

It is noteworthy that U.S. president Woodrow Wilson, a Christian and a Bible student, sent this protest against the arbitrary act of partition:

> The Zionist cause is tied to the security of Biblical boundaries and
> has in view the economic development of the country. This means

that in the north Palestine should reach to the River Litani and the
source of the streams of Mount Hermon; in the east it should include
the plains of Jaulon and Haran. Otherwise we would have a case of
mutilation. I would like to remind you that neither Washington nor
Paris have manifested opposition to the Zionist plan nor to securing
indispensable Biblical boundaries.[7]

Winston Churchill's concessions to the Arabs did not put an end
to their opposition, which was manifested in continued rioting and
acts of terrorism. Sometimes the British Army suppressed these Arab
riots; at other times they were quelled by the Jewish self-defense
organization, the *Haganah*.

In 1929, Arabs rioted over the issue of Jews praying at the Wail-
ing Wall and then massacred seventy defenseless Jews in Hebron
on the Sabbath. After that, the Haganah usually trained a corps of
volunteers to protect small isolated settlements. In later years, the
British armed "peace bands" of moderate Arabs in order to help
protect the country from roving Arab terrorist bands.

Struggles, Conflicts, Progress

In spite of all these difficulties, Jewish development continued to
flourish. Young Jewish Zionists from eastern Europe immigrated in
large numbers immediately after the Balfour Declaration.

In the mid-1920s, middle-class artisans and shopkeepers arrived
to settle the towns and cities and to build factories, shops, hotels
and restaurants. Construction and road building became major
industries. The Jewish National Fund, using money provided by
Zionist organizations in other countries, bought up sizable tracts
of land for settlement. The General Federation of Jewish Labor,
the *Histadrut*, was founded in 1922. Within the Histadrut, leader-
ship emerged that was destined to form Israel's first government
in 1948.

From the time of partition in 1922, no Jewish immigration was
permitted to eastern Palestine—i.e., Transjordan. No such restric-
tions, however, were placed on Arab immigration to the Jewish

homeland. Arabs entered freely to take advantage of the higher wages and living standards resulting from Jewish development. In fact, while the Jewish population rose by 375,000 between World War I and World War II, the non-Jewish population increased by 380,000. Interestingly enough, the Arab increase was largest in areas of intensive Jewish development (e.g., a 216 percent increase in Haifa) and negligible where there was little Jewish influx.

Hitler's rise to power in Germany in 1933 caused much of the Jewish immigration. By 1936, more than 164,000 new settlers had reached Palestine. Some of them were able to bring in substantial amounts of capital for investment. Absentee Arab landlords took advantage of the situation and sold swampy, rocky or sandy soil at exorbitant prices. Jews paid more than $20 million to Arab landowners between 1933 and 1935. Then they drained the swamps, watered the deserts and planted trees and crops. Although most of the Jewish people had been away from the soil for centuries, when they returned to their homeland, they developed unparalleled skill for making the barren land produce abundant crops.

Mounting tension between Jews and Arabs through the 1930s created additional tension between the new Jewish immigrants and the British mandatory government. Although there was an element of strong pro-Zionist public opinion in Britain, considerations of expediency often caused the government to attempt to appease the Arabs.

When World War II broke out in 1939, almost the entire Jewish population between the ages of 18 and 50—136,000 persons in all—volunteered immediately for the British Army. The British selected only a few hundred specialists at that time, but by the end of the war, more than 26,000 Jews from Palestine were serving in the Jewish Brigade. Fighting a common enemy strengthened British-Jewish ties, especially when most Arabs in Palestine were indifferent or pro-Nazi. The Arab mufti of Jerusalem, in particular, was openly pro-Nazi and visited Germany in 1941 to offer Arab assistance in the Nazi "final solution to the Jewish problem."

The large military force in the Middle East during most of World War II helped the Jewish economy in Palestine. Agricultural productivity increased, especially as new Jewish settlements developed in the more fertile parts of the country. Industry and technology in war-related materials flourished. For both Jews and Arabs, it was a time of quiet, somewhat like the eye in the center of a hurricane. When World War II ended, currents began to swirl again, which have not yet abated.

3

BIRTH PAINS
OF A NATION

The destiny of the Jewish community in Palestine, and ultimately of the entire Jewish people worldwide, hung in the balance from 1946 to 1948. Up to the time of my discharge from the British Army in April 1946, I had been an interested but passive spectator of the situation developing in Palestine. While deeply stirred by the way I saw various aspects of Bible prophecy being fulfilled before my eyes, I had no thought of becoming actively involved. The providence of God, however, decreed otherwise.

For a while after my discharge, Lydia and I continued to live with our girls in Ramallah. Soon, however, our Arab neighbors made it clear that they were no longer willing to tolerate Jewish girls living in their midst. We had no alternative but to move to Jerusalem before the hatred burning in our neighbors' eyes erupted into acts of violence against the girls.

In Jerusalem, the tension was increasing steadily. Sabotage by Jewish underground organizations provoked retaliation and repression by the British military forces. Armed clashes tore the uneasy peace. Arab snipers armed with rifles stationed themselves on rooftops or other vantage points and shot indiscriminately at passersby. At night the streets grew dark and deserted, and no one dared to go out.

In spite of the prevailing tensions, I was able to enroll as a postgraduate student at the Hebrew University, then located on Mount Scopus, close to the place I had concluded my military service. With sporadic interruptions, I was able to continue my studies there for the next eighteen months.

Effects of Partition

On November 29, 1947, the United Nations voted to partition Palestine into two separate states, one Jewish and one Arab. From this point on, the situation in Jerusalem degenerated rapidly into a state of undeclared war. Jews and Arabs were no longer willing to live side by side. The city was split into a number of armed camps, some controlled by Jews and others by Arabs.

Officially, the British were still responsible for the maintenance of law and order. The military forces they had at their disposal were more than sufficient to enable them to carry out their task effectively.

To my dismay, they chose not to do this. Instead, they openly tolerated—and even at times supported—the looting and murder carried out by armed bands of Arabs against Jews. They also used their military superiority to prevent the Jews from acquiring the weapons they needed to defend themselves. With my firsthand knowledge of the methods of the British Army, I could come to only one conclusion: *My country's official representatives in Palestine at that time were doing everything in their power, short of open war, to prevent the emergence of the state of Israel.*

One major element in the "security forces" under the direction of the British was the Arab Legion. This was the official military force of Transjordan (later renamed Jordan)—trained, equipped, financed and commanded by the British. So far as the Jewish people were concerned, however, the Arab Legion offered them no security whatever. On the contrary, it was the most powerful of the various Arab forces aligned against them.

On the evening of December 12, 1947, through a conversation providentially overheard by one of our girls, we learned that a truck full of armed soldiers from the Arab Legion was making preparations to attack our house. Since we had no protection against this kind of "security," our whole family simply filed out into the dark, deserted streets of Jerusalem. After wandering for two hours, we found refuge for the night in an American Christian mission. In the morning, the Muslim Arabs in the neighborhood of this mission sent word to the missionary in charge that if he continued to harbor our Jewish girls, they would burn the building down. Twenty-four hours later, we again found ourselves refugees in the streets of Jerusalem.

For the next two months, we lived the life of refugees, until we were eventually invited to move into a large mission building in the main Jewish area of Jerusalem. The missionaries who had occupied it were leaving the country and wished us to take charge of the building in their absence. There we remained through the months that saw the birth of the state of Israel.

Jerusalem Besieged

By this time, the Jewish area of Jerusalem had become a city under siege. All communication with the Arab communities that lay to the north, east and south had ceased. To the west, roving, semimilitary bands of Arabs had cut the route to Tel Aviv and the coastal area.

The British did nothing to restrain these Arab bands. Instead, they used their forces to prevent the Jews from taking any effective steps to reopen the road between Tel Aviv and Jerusalem. Consequently, the area in which we lived was deprived of almost all food supplies and was on the verge of starvation.

On May 14, 1948, the British forces finally withdrew from Palestine, and the state of Israel was officially proclaimed. The very next day, all the surrounding Arab nations declared war on Israel and commenced full-scale military operations against it, with the declared intention of destroying the new state. A total of more than 40 million people, with modern, well-equipped armies, were thus at war with a tiny, newborn nation of less than 640,000 people, whose volunteer army had been assembled at 48 hours' notice, with no equipment except a random assortment of light arms.

On May 17, the Arab Legion started to shell the Jewish section of Jerusalem with heavy artillery. The first shell exploded only yards from the building in which we were living. A large, jagged fragment flew through an open window, passed directly between two of our girls and battered a hole about two inches deep in the opposite wall. Both girls were knocked down by the blast. When the shell fragment was cool enough to handle, I picked it up and examined it. It consisted of nearly half the base of the shell. Neatly imprinted on it were the words "Made in Britain."

The Arab Legion continued their shelling of Jerusalem for almost a month, as casualties mounted among the civilian population. The Arabs made no attempt to confine their fire to what might have been considered military objectives. They rained shells at random on hospitals, churches and diplomatic buildings, even though these were marked clearly with the appropriate insignia.

Early in June, the United Nations succeeded in imposing a temporary cease-fire in Palestine. For four weeks, this halted full-scale fighting, although sniping and sporadic minor clashes continued. I took advantage of the cease-fire to write a letter to the vice chancellor of Cambridge University (who happened to be a personal friend), in which I described events in Palestine as I had witnessed them over the past six months. I asked him to use his good offices to bring the situation to the attention of both the government and the press.

My letter closed with this summary:

What I have written above, I have written out of a profound
conviction . . . that deserves to be plainly stated and widely
known. . . . I can sum up my conclusions in four sentences:

(1) Since November 1947, the British Government has systematically resisted the implementation of the United Nations decision concerning Palestine and the setting up of a Jewish state.

(2) Within Palestine, the present policy of the British Government is calculated to increase the possibility of prolonged and heavy fighting.

(3) Outside Palestine, the effect of British policy is to undermine the United Nations Organisation.

(4) The indiscriminate shelling of Jerusalem, continued for twenty-seven days and nights, is—in all but name—a British military operation.

In closing, let me give utterance to two questions that now form themselves daily in my mind: Do the people of Britain know what is being done in their name in Palestine? If so, are they satisfied about it?

At this stage, however, all regular mail service out of the country had ceased; and by the time my letter reached the vice chancellor, it was too late for him to make any effective use of the information.

A Nation Born in a Day

When the four-week cease-fire ended, full-scale fighting resumed immediately. In the intervening period, both Jews and Arabs had consolidated their positions and brought in additional supplies. There had also been another kind of change in the situation, however—one that could not be explained merely in terms of military supplies or strategy.

It was one of those intangible, indefinable factors in human affairs that are not recorded in official histories. Yet its effect was decisive. From the new perspective I had gained since coming to Israel, I saw it as the outworking of the most powerful force in human affairs—the prophetic Word of God. By all accepted standards, the odds against Israel were still overwhelming. Yet I watched in awe as the tide of war turned against the Arab armies—slowly at first, but unmistakably. By the end of 1948, virtually all the invading Arab armies had been forced to withdraw, and the state of Israel was established within borders somewhat larger than those originally proposed by the United Nations. (See the back of this book for a chronology of events from 1947 to 2004.)

Undoubtedly, further conflicts and tremendous sacrifices still lay ahead; but one fact of paramount importance overshadowed all else: *The state of Israel had been born and had survived.*

Once again, I found in the words of one of Israel's prophets a summary of the events I had witnessed. The account, written thousands of years earlier, could not be surpassed for its vividness or for the way it focused precisely on those features that were unique:

> "Who has ever heard of such a thing?
> Who has ever seen such things?
> Can a country be born in a day
> or a nation be brought forth in a moment?
> Yet no sooner is Zion in labor
> than she gives birth to her children."
>
> Isaiah 66:8

That was exactly what I had been permitted to see with my own eyes! On one day—May 14, 1948—Israel was born as a complete nation, with its own government, armed forces and necessary administrative functions. True, everything had been improvised hastily and on a small scale. Yet all the necessary ingredients were there to make Israel a sovereign nation within its own borders. So far as I knew, such an event was without parallel in human history.

Our final year in Jerusalem, 1948, was fraught with much hardship and danger, but we all survived without personal injury. Toward the end of that year, Lydia and I moved with our family to Britain. In retrospect, we recognized that all we had gone through was a small price to pay for the privilege of witnessing perhaps the most important fulfillment of biblical prophecy since the first century.

Retrospect from Britain

In my native land once again after an absence of seven years, I reflected further on the role Britain had played in the closing period of the mandate in Palestine. I am British by birth and grateful for my heritage. It gives me no satisfaction to record the misdeeds of Britain's official representatives.

Nevertheless, I believe it is important that the facts be stated clearly, because there are significant lessons to be learned—lessons that could benefit other nations and governments today.

As indicated in the previous chapter, the people of Britain made a unique contribution to the establishment of the state of Israel. For more than three centuries, Christians in Britain had nourished a vision, based on the Bible, that God desired to make of the Jewish people a sovereign nation once again in their own land.

Politically, this vision found expression through such men as Lord Shaftesbury and Lord Balfour. In 1917, it was the Balfour Declaration, made on behalf of the British government, that set into motion the political processes that issued in the establishment of the state of Israel 31 years later. It was the British government, too, that took the decisive step of placing before the United Nations the future of Palestine.

After all this, it amounted to inconsistency and hypocrisy of the highest order for the same British government to attempt to undermine the decision of the United Nations by resisting the establishment of the state of Israel. Such conduct tarnished the reputation of Britain and proved to be the first stage of a prolonged national decline.

This shift in British policy at a crucial moment in the history of the Middle East came about without any official decision of the British Parliament and without the majority of the British public being aware of what was taking place. What were the factors that contributed to such a shift? Two were clearly discernible.

First, there were calculations—never publicly formulated—of economic and political expediency. As early as 1939, it had become clear that the world would soon face a shortage of oil. At the same time, the economies of all the developed nations were becoming more and more dependent each year on ever-increasing supplies of oil. A major share of the world's store of oil was controlled by the Arab nations of the Middle East. The disavowed goal of British policy was to continue offering lip service to the Balfour Declaration but at the same time to gain favor with the Arabs by underhanded activities aimed at sabotaging the emerging Jewish state.

Second, latent elements of anti-Semitism were festering among the British and surfaced at this juncture. As with the calculations concerning oil, these anti-Semitic sentiments were not, for the most part, given official expression (although some utterances by military commanders must be excepted). Nevertheless, sentiments of this kind influenced critical decisions on policy and, still more, the practical application of policy.

The people who yielded to such sentiments—and gave such direction to British policy regarding the Middle East—overlooked one important fact: *There is a moral and spiritual force at work in the destinies of nations.* The responsibility of government goes beyond mere calculations of economic or military expedience. To sacrifice moral and spiritual principles on such an altar will never serve the best interests of any nation. Ironically, the calculations that prompt this kind of conduct ultimately yield results opposite to those intended.

An illustration of this principle comes from Exodus. The Israelites were aliens in Egypt, their fate determined largely by the pharaoh who occupied the throne. At a certain point, a new and despotic king came to power with a new "Jewish policy." He proclaimed it as follows:

> "Look," he said to his people, "the Israelites have become much too numerous for us. Come, we must deal shrewdly with them or they will become even more numerous and, if war breaks out, will join our enemies, fight against us and leave the country."
>
> Exodus 1:9–10

This new king reversed the policy of his predecessors and oppressed the Israelites. The record goes on to show, however, that his "shrewd dealing" could not ultimately prevent the outworking of God's purpose for Israel. His policy only proved disastrous for Egypt. Such is the end of "expediency" that opposes the revealed purposes of God. A single verse in Proverbs succinctly states the futility of opposing the purposes of God: "There is no wisdom, no insight, no plan that can succeed against the LORD" (Proverbs 21:30).

Likewise, a single verse in Job reveals that the destiny of every nation is determined ultimately by God: "He makes nations great, and destroys them; he enlarges nations, and disperses them" (Job 12:23).

For any nation or government, it is expedient to gain the favor of almighty God, but it is extremely inexpedient to incur His disfavor.

PART II

Prophetic Fulfillment

4

GOD'S PREDETERMINED PLAN

I f the birth of Israel was miraculous, the growth of that tiny
new state was equally so. In its first decade, this infant nation
of less than 640,000 absorbed more than twice that number of
new immigrants, many of them refugees. It housed them, clothed
them, fed them, taught them the Hebrew language, trained them
and placed them in jobs. Even with such rapid internal growth,
Israel built up its defense forces and held at bay hostile Arab nations on all sides.

It is outside the scope of this book to provide a detailed history
of the state of Israel. Yet it is impossible to comprehend the magni-
tude of the pressures under which Israel presently exists without
an overall awareness of the events that have taken place since 1948.
For readers unfamiliar with this period of Israel's history, therefore, I
have prepared a brief chronology, which can be found in the special
section at the back of this book.

The pressures to which Israel has continuously been subjected are possibly without parallel in history: hostile neighbors, 5 wars, terrorism, inflation, media misrepresentation, economic boycott. This tiny nation with a population of 6 million, of whom just under 5 million are Jewish, occupies an area just over 8,000 square miles. In contrast, its hostile Arab neighbors number more than 150 million people, living on 5 million square miles. The armies of the Arab League number nearly 1 million men, contrasted with Israel's 164,000. (See special section.)

Nevertheless, the nation has continued to grow and flourish. In the face of all their pressures, the Israelis plant and harvest, build and manufacture, and develop their culture. Behind this lies one inescapable fact: *Israel's survival is at stake.* The same imponderable supernatural force that brought the nation to birth continues to preserve and uphold it. Simply stated, each day that Israel continues to exist represents one more miracle.

As we have already seen, the key to understanding this miracle—as well as the whole critical situation of the Middle East—can be found in the prophetic revelation of the Bible. It is in the Middle East that history and the Bible intersect. This has been true for four thousand years, but never more so than today.

The central theme of biblical prophecy, as it is being unfolded in our time, revolves around the land and the people of Israel. God is carrying out His predetermined plan to regather the Jewish people from their worldwide dispersion and restore them to their ancient homeland.

The best way to comprehend this plan is to let God's Word speak for itself. In the Bible, God Himself has already spoken *the last word on the Middle East.*

"In That Day"

Isaiah the prophet paints a comprehensive picture of the regathering of Israel "from the four quarters of the earth":

In that day the Root of Jesse will stand as a banner for the peoples; the nations will rally to him, and his place of rest will be glorious. In that day the Lord will reach out his hand a second time to reclaim the remnant that is left of his people from Assyria, from Lower Egypt, from Upper Egypt, from Cush, from Elam, from Babylonia, from Hamath and from the islands of the sea.

> He will raise a banner for the nations
>   and gather the exiles of Israel;
> he will assemble the scattered people of Judah
>   from the four quarters of the earth.
> Ephraim's jealousy will vanish,
>   and Judah's enemies will be cut off;
> Ephraim will not be jealous of Judah,
>   nor Judah hostile toward Ephraim.
> They will swoop down on the slopes of Philistia to the west;
>   together they will plunder the people to the east.
> They will lay hands on Edom and Moab,
>   and the Ammonites will be subject to them.

Isaiah 11:10–14

In the forefront of his picture, in verse 10, Isaiah introduces "the Root of Jesse"—one of the main biblical titles of the Messiah. Isaiah here predicts that the Messiah will stand as a banner for the peoples, the nations (Gentiles) will rally to Him and His place of rest will be glorious.

All these predictions have been fulfilled in Jesus of Nazareth. After completing His earthly ministry, Jesus returned to His place of rest in the glory of God the Father. Since then, He has become a "banner" to whom people all over the world have looked. Many of these have "rallied" to Him; that is, they have acknowledged Him as Savior and Lord and have become His disciples.

In both verses 10 and 11, there occurs a key expression: "in that day." Altogether in the prophet Isaiah, the expression *in that day* occurs nearly fifty times—usually in relation to the Messiah. It does not always necessarily indicate a single specific period in human history. Rather, it implies that *that day* is where the Messiah is. In other words, the Messiah creates around Himself a specific period of time.

There can be no doubt, however, that in many places in Isaiah, the expression *that day* refers to a period of time near the close of the present age. In this present context, I believe both interpretations apply.

A Second Regathering

> In that day the Lord will reach out his hand a second time to reclaim the remnant that is left of his people from Assyria, from Lower Egypt, from Upper Egypt, from Cush, from Elam, from Babylonia, from Hamath and from the islands of the sea.
>
> verse 11

This verse out of Isaiah 11 is particularly significant—in part because of a widely held theory that the book of Isaiah is the work of more than one prophet. This theory gives rise to expressions such as "second Isaiah," "third Isaiah" and so on. For my part, I find no logical basis for this theory. Some interpreters of the Bible, however, assume *a priori* that it is not possible for a prophet of God to predict future events in detail and with complete accuracy.

One example of such a prediction is found in Isaiah 44 and 45, in which the prophet names Cyrus as the ruler who would open the way for the return of the Jews from Babylon to Jerusalem. Because Cyrus is mentioned here by name, some recent Bible interpreters have concluded that the passage must have been written by a later prophet who was a contemporary of Cyrus.

I do not accept this line of reasoning as valid, however, because I believe in God's total omniscience. That is, it is perfectly possible for a prophet of God to predict events in the distant future accurately and in detail. I do not need to believe that such predictions were written after the event by another person claiming to be a prophet and then were attributed to a period before the event. This would be deliberate deception, and I do not believe there is any deception in the prophetic Word of God.

There is an interesting piece of corollary evidence in the Dead Sea Scrolls, which date to within the first century BC or AD and which can be seen in the Israeli Museum in Jerusalem. On display is a complete scroll of the prophet Isaiah, written in parallel columns—from top to bottom and from right to left.

Most of the interpreters who attribute Isaiah to more than one prophet make their main division at the end of chapter 39. In this particular manuscript, chapter 39 happens to end one line from the bottom of the column. In such a case, if the scribe had thought that a new prophet was beginning with chapter 40, it would have been natural for him to leave the bottom line of this column blank and move on to the next column.

But he did not do this. In other words, a scribe from this early period did not entertain the idea that Isaiah represented the work of more than one prophet. I find no reason to entertain it, either.

Back in Isaiah 11, well before the Babylonian captivity, the prophet foresees the Jewish people scattered from their land and then regathered to it—*not once, but twice.* ("In that day the Lord will reach out his hand a second time to reclaim the remnant that is left of his people.") He looks *beyond* the Babylonian captivity and the return to Jerusalem and sees a second scattering and a second regathering—the one that primarily concerns us here.

The list of places from which the second regathering will take place is important: Assyria (now mainly Iraq); lower and upper Egypt (that is, the whole of modern Egypt); Cush (sometimes identified as Ethiopia); Elam (now Iran, or Persia); Babylonia (once again, mainly Iraq); Hamath (Syria); and the islands—or coastlands—of the sea. (This word translated *islands* can be understood to refer to all the other areas of the earth that border on the ocean—that is, what today we call "continents.")

The Jews' return from Babylonian captivity did not constitute a complete fulfillment of this prediction, since it specifies countries and areas of the earth from which no Jews at that time returned. The prophet is looking forward, in other words, to a further scattering of Israel after the Babylonian captivity and then to a further regathering after this second scattering.

It is significant to note that this prediction occurs so early in Isaiah's prophecy.

A Banner for the Nations

Isaiah now reveals one main purpose of God that is to be accomplished by this second regathering of Israel:

> He [the Lord] will raise a banner for the nations
>   and gather the exiles of Israel;
> he will assemble the scattered people of Judah
>   from the four quarters of the earth.
>
> verse 12

Isaiah reemphasizes that this second regathering is to take place *from every quarter of the globe*—a prediction that was not nearly fulfilled by the return from Babylon. In this context, the prophet says, "He [the Lord] will raise a banner for the nations." It is important to understand that the regathering of Israel to their own land in our time is a *banner* the Lord has raised for the nations.

How shall we interpret this metaphor of a "banner"? First, a banner is something displayed publicly, often lifted above the level of surrounding objects, in order to attract attention. Second, a banner usually conveys some brief, specific message. There can be no doubt that the regathering of Israel has fulfilled the first function of a banner—to attract the attention of the other nations.

This was brought home to me most forcefully in the summer of 1979 when my second wife, Ruth, and I spent three months studying at the Hebrew University in Jerusalem. We observed that, throughout those months, there was not one week in which Israel was not the focus of world news. Here was a nation with less than 4 million people (at that time), in a territory so small there is scarcely room for its name on a map of the world; yet every week it made front-page headlines around the globe.

About that time, the United States terminated its treaty with Taiwan and entered into a relationship with Communist China, a nation with almost 1 billion people. This created a stir in the world press that lasted scarcely a month, and then people forgot about the whole thing again. Yet the situation involved more than a quarter of the world's population!

Israel, on the other hand, with a population of less than half of one percent of that of Communist China, remains continuously at the center of world interest.

This is no accident. God has raised a banner for the nations. He has gained their attention and is now speaking to them through it. What is He saying? I believe God intends to focus the attention of the world on two things: His Word and His covenant.

Concerning His Word, God is saying to the nations, "The Bible, My Word, is a true, relevant, up-to-date Book. Its predictions are still being fulfilled today with absolute accuracy."

Concerning His covenant, God is saying, "I am a God who keeps My covenant. Four thousand years ago, I made a covenant with Abraham and with his descendants after him. I promised never to break that covenant, and I have never broken it. That covenant is still in force today, and I am now causing it to be worked out through the course of human history."

The whole world needs to understand two important facts. First, the Bible is the Book with the answer to today's problems. Second, when God makes a covenant, it stands fast. In the midst of a culture and a society in which words have become virtually meaningless, compromise belongs to the order of the day and people no longer take promises or commitments seriously, we need to be reminded that God has given promises in Scripture that He will never forget. He has served notice to all nations that He keeps His covenant and watches over His Word to bring it to fulfillment.

He is a God exalted above all nations, who carries out unerringly those decisions He has caused to be recorded in Scripture. Any nation that ignores God's Word does so to its own great loss.

Victories of Regathered Israel

Isaiah's prophecy goes on to point out one important difference between regathered Israel and the condition of the nation before it was first carried off into exile:

> Ephraim's jealousy will vanish,
> and Judah's enemies will be cut off;
> Ephraim will not be jealous of Judah,
> nor Judah hostile toward Ephraim.

verse 13

Bear in mind that the Israel of Isaiah's day had been split into two kingdoms: the northern kingdom, which is usually called Israel, or Ephraim; and the southern kingdom, called Judah. Most of the time these two kingdoms were at war with one another, producing a condition of disunity and instability that made them prey to invading Gentile empires. First, the northern kingdom was taken into exile by Assyria. Then, a little more than one hundred years later, the southern kingdom was taken into exile by Babylon.

This gives added significance to Isaiah's prediction. Israel went into exile as a divided nation. But when the final restoration takes place, Israel will be once more a single, united nation. All rivalry will have ceased.

In this respect, too, history followed the course indicated by prophecy. Until just a short while before Israel was reborn as a nation in 1948, no official name had been chosen for the new state. In fact, choosing a name became something of a crisis. One name that was proposed and almost accepted was "Judea." At the last moment, however, the choice was made for "Israel."

This choice confirmed the fulfillment of Isaiah's prophecy. Historically, "Judea" has applied only to the southern kingdom and would, therefore, have implied a continuation of the division into two rival nations. "Israel," on the other hand, is the correct biblical name for the total nation descended from Abraham, Isaac and Jacob. The choice of this name signaled the reuniting of the two divided kingdoms. Here is another example of the detailed outworking of prophecy in history.

The prophetic picture of Israel's regathering continues:

> They will swoop down on the slopes of Philistia to the west;
> together they will plunder the people to the east.

They will lay hands on Edom and Moab,
and the Ammonites will be subject to them.

verse 14

I have already pointed out that the biblical words *Philistia* and *Philistine* are the roots from which are derived the contemporary words *Palestine* and *Palestinian*. The first part of verse 14, read in this way, tells us that the regathered nation of Israel will swoop down on the slopes of Philistia (the Palestinians) to the west—that is, toward Gaza and the Sinai.

Without commenting on the political implications of this statement, we have to acknowledge that this is precisely what has taken place. Isaiah also says that the Israelites will then turn toward the east, and he mentions three place names: Edom, Moab and Ammon. In our day, these three places are all found within the boundaries of one nation: Jordan.

Someone once remarked that the Jordan is a strange river—it is the only one in the world that has only one bank. At least, the West Bank is the only one ever mentioned in the news! In this passage, however, God is speaking about the East Bank. I am not making any predictions, but the Bible seems to indicate that instead of the Palestinians taking over the West Bank, the Israelis will in due course establish some kind of governmental control over the East Bank.

You may say, "That is not what the experts anticipate." Frankly, that does not disturb me! There is no situation in modern history about which the "experts" have been so consistently wrong as the reestablishment of Israel.

God Works through Suffering

In Isaiah 43, the prophet again takes up this theme of Israel's restoration:

But now, this is what the LORD says—
he who created you, O Jacob,
he who formed you, O Israel:

"Fear not, for I have redeemed you;
 I have summoned you by name; you are mine.
When you pass through the waters,
 I will be with you;
and when you pass through the rivers,
 they will not sweep over you.
When you walk through the fire,
 you will not be burned;
 the flames will not set you ablaze.
For I am the LORD, your God,
 the Holy One of Israel, your Savior;
I give Egypt for your ransom,
 Cush and Seba in your stead.
Since you are precious and honored in my sight,
 and because I love you,
I will give men in exchange for you,
 and people in exchange for your life.
Do not be afraid, for I am with you;
 I will bring your children from the east
 and gather you from the west.
I will say to the north, 'Give them up!'
 and to the south, 'Do not hold them back.'
Bring my sons from afar
 and my daughters from the ends of the earth—
everyone who is called by my name,
 whom I created for my glory,
 whom I formed and made."

Isaiah 43:1–7

The previous chapter, Isaiah 42, ends with a description of Israel's rebellion against God and of the severe judgment that came upon them as a consequence. Chapter 43 begins with the word *but*, indicating a difference in the way God now intends to deal with Israel—a change from judgment to mercy.

In that first verse of chapter 43, God uses two different words to describe the way He deals with Israel: to "create" and to "form." To create describes the initial act of bringing something into being, but to form describes making something the way we desire it to be. This latter expression suggests particularly the work of a potter. First, God *created* Israel, but now He is in the process of *forming* Israel.

> "When you pass through the waters,
>   I will be with you;
> and when you pass through the rivers,
>   they will not sweep over you.
> When you walk through the fire,
>   you will not be burned;
>   the flames will not set you ablaze."
>
> verse 2

Again we see the accuracy of biblical prophecy. The vivid phrases of this verse depict the history of the Jewish people through a period of almost 2,000 years. They have indeed passed through the rivers and walked through the fire. There is only one explanation of their continued survival as a people: *God has been with them.*

> "For I am the LORD, your God,
>   the Holy One of Israel, your Savior;
> I give Egypt for your ransom,
>   Cush and Seba in your stead.
> Since you are precious and honored in my sight,
>   and because I love you,
> I will give men in exchange for you,
>   and people in exchange for your life."
>
> verses 3–4

These verses contain a revelation of tremendous importance. We need to recognize the values God sets on things and people, because they are so unlike the values promoted by the humanistic philosophy of our time.

Notice, as a biblical parallel, the story of Job. God, in His dealings with Job, was prepared to give his seven sons and three daughters over to death. God set such great value on this one man, in other words, that He sacrificed all Job's children.

You and I do not think this way. God's values are different from ours. The story of Job reveals how much suffering God is willing to permit in order to accomplish His purpose with just one man.

However, the story does not end with suffering. Once Job learned his lesson and came to understand God more fully, God gave back to Job exactly double all that he had at first: twice as many camels, twice as many donkeys, twice as much gold and silver.

When it came to Job's children, however, God gave him back only as many as he had originally. Why? Because Job's first children were not lost; God had merely taken them to Himself. They had gone on ahead of Job. What a precious revelation!

I do not believe that we can understand human history, especially in this century, until we realize that God is prepared to let terrible things happen in order to accomplish His purpose with one particular nation: Israel. God warned Israel of the terrible sufferings they would pass through, but in the midst of it all He gave them this wonderful assurance: "Since you are precious and honored in my sight, and because I love you, I will give men in exchange for you, and people in exchange for your life."

When God declares His love, He says "because," but He does not say "why." He tells Israel, "I will do this for you because I love you." But He never says *why* He loves Israel.

We as Christians have come to accept this unexplained love of God as the bedrock of our faith. We believe that God was willing to offer the spotless Lamb of God, Jesus Christ, to die on the cross for our sins. There was nothing in any of us to merit this sacrifice. Jesus did not die for us because we deserved it. He did it for one reason only: *because He loves us.*

For the Church, as for Israel, there is a depth and a sovereignty in the love of God for which He never offers a reason. Yet it is the ultimate motivation for everything God does for us, whether for an individual or a whole nation.

Interwoven with the mystery of God's sovereign love is the mystery of the suffering that He permits His loved ones to endure. Later, the prophet Isaiah continues the theme of Israel's suffering: "See, I have refined you, though not as silver; I have tested you in the furnace of affliction" (Isaiah 48:10).

God permits those He loves to pass through suffering, because the end result is of infinite value in His sight, and it cannot be achieved in any other way.

Regathered from All Lands

In Isaiah 43:3–4, God has declared that His love for Israel will influence His dealings with other nations. Now He goes on to describe how His intervention will also affect Israel directly:

> "Do not be afraid, for I am with you;
>> I will bring your children from the east
>> and gather you from the west.
> I will say to the north, 'Give them up!'
>> and to the south, 'Do not hold them back.'
> Bring my sons from afar
>> and my daughters from the ends of the earth—
> everyone who is called by my name,
>> whom I created for my glory,
>> whom I formed and made."
>
> Isaiah 43:5–7

Once again, God speaks of regathering Israel from all four quarters of the compass. (Clearly this prediction, like that in Isaiah 11, was not fulfilled by the return from Babylon.) God here reveals that His sovereign choice is the determining factor in human history. He says to Israel, "I have put My name upon you; therefore you shall be Mine. All that I work out in history, I do because I have chosen you."

In the last resort, the destiny of nations—like that of individuals—will be determined by their response to God's sovereign choice. How perfectly Isaiah's language applies to the contemporary regathering of Israel from the various parts of the world! The prophet uses different verbs to describe the process by which God regathers Israel from each of the four points of the compass.

In verse 5, God says, "I will *bring* your children from the east, and *gather* you from the west." We must keep in mind that each of the directions mentioned is given in relation to the land of Israel. "The east," therefore, refers primarily to Asia. "The west" indicates mainly North and South America and, in particular, the great concentration of Jewish people in the United States.

The verbs used here do not indicate any particular opposition to the Jewish people leaving either the east or the west. In fact, with particular regard to the west, there seems to be a suggestion of reluctance on their part to leave. All this corresponds accurately to recent history.

When we read on in verse 6, however, the verbs used for Israel's regathering present a different picture: "I will say to the north, 'Give them up!' and to the south, 'Do not hold them back.'" As we have seen earlier, "north" includes Germany, Poland and Russia. Russia, the largest of these nations, also has the largest concentration of Jews remaining within her borders. The sudden and unexpected fall of the Soviet Union and its satellites showed that where Russia resisted, God was determined to make a way. Since the fall of state communism, almost 1 million Jews have returned to Israel from the former Soviet Union. This makes God's words to the north particularly appropriate: "Give them up!"

Likewise, the words spoken to the south, "Do not hold them back," indicate possible unwillingness on the part of those addressed. The Hebrew word here translated *south* actually denotes the country of Yemen. Again, the choice of the verb is appropriate. Yemen is a fanatically Muslim country, strongly opposed to the state of Israel. Who would have believed that a country like this would have released almost its entire Jewish population, numbering nearly 50,000, shortly after Israel became a state? Yet this is what happened (see special section, p. 146). Once again, we see both the accuracy and the authority of Scripture.

Judgment Makes Way for Mercy

Isaiah 43 ends with a further reminder of Israel's rebellion and of the judgment that rebellion has brought upon them. Then chapter

44 opens with the words "but now," again indicating the transition from judgment to mercy:

> "But now listen, O Jacob, my servant,
>   Israel, whom I have chosen.
> This is what the LORD says—
>   he who made you, who formed you in the womb,
>   and who will help you:
> Do not be afraid, O Jacob, my servant,
>   Jeshurun, whom I have chosen."
>
> Isaiah 44:1–2

Twice in these verses we find the phrase "Israel, whom I have chosen," reemphasizing that God's dealings with Israel are based on His sovereign choice, not on Israel's merits. Another recurrent theme of this chapter is represented by phrases such as "Do not be afraid" and "Do not tremble." When we consider all the dangers the Jewish people have passed through in the process of restoration to their own land, and those dangers that still confront them on every side, we can readily understand how timely that word of encouragement is.

Then God reveals the spiritual climax He has in mind:

> "For I will pour water on the thirsty land,
>   and streams on the dry ground;
> I will pour out my Spirit on your offspring,
>   and my blessing on your descendants."
>
> verse 3

The initial phases of Israel's restoration have been mainly political and geographical. The Bible consistently emphasizes, however, that the end purpose is spiritual. God will not conclude the process of restoration that He set into motion until He has fulfilled His spiritual purpose, which is the outpouring of His Spirit.

Further on in the same chapter, God affirms the absolute certainty of the promises He has given to Israel:

"This is what the LORD says—
your Redeemer, who formed you in the womb:

I am the LORD,
who has made all things,
who alone stretched out the heavens,
who spread out the earth by myself,

who foils the signs of false prophets
   and makes fools of diviners,
who overthrows the learning of the wise
   and turns it into nonsense,
who carries out the words of his servants
   and fulfills the predictions of his messengers."

verses 24–26

Here God declares Himself to be the great Creator who maintains sovereign control over all He has created. In particular, when God speaks a word through His servants the prophets, He watches over that word and sees that it comes to complete fulfillment.

On the other hand, a word from any other source that is spoken in opposition to God's Word will not come to fulfillment but will be overthrown. This applies especially to the words of false prophets and diviners. God will bring them to naught.

Diviners and False Prophets

The word *diviners* denotes all who seek to predict future events by resorting to occult sources. This includes the countless forms of this "art" so prevalent today—astrology (including horoscopes), palmistry, card reading, séances, ouija boards and many others. God warns that all who rely on such activities are doomed to ultimate deception and frustration.

Isaiah's declaration that God will overthrow the words of false prophets applies in a special, practical way to the current situation in the Middle East. The strongest spiritual force that opposes God's purposes and God's people in the Middle East today is Islam, the Mohammedan religion. Yet Mohammed, the founder of Islam, was a false prophet. As such, his words and the movement he brought into being will ultimately be brought to naught.

Some may be inclined to challenge the statement that Mohammed was a false prophet. To this I would offer one brief and simple response: *If Jesus was a true prophet, then Mohammed was a false prophet.* Following are a few of the main points in which the teaching of Mohammed contradicts that of Jesus.

1. Jesus declared that He was the Son of God. Islam totally rejects the idea that God can have a son, dismissing it as blasphemy. Islam further rejects the concept of one God revealed in three Persons.
2. Historically, the Christian faith has centered on the crucifixion and resurrection of Jesus. Islam denies that Jesus ever actually died on the cross or that He was resurrected.
3. Jesus claimed He had come to fulfill the Law and the prophets (see Matthew 5:17). Islam claims that it alone is the true fulfillment and completion of the revelation contained in the Old and New Testaments.
4. Jesus promised His followers that He would send them another "Comforter" (see John 14:16–17, 26, KJV). The Christian Church has always taught that this promise was fulfilled by the coming of the Holy Spirit on the Day of Pentecost. Islam claims that Mohammed was the Comforter promised by Jesus.
5. The Old Testament, which Jesus accepted as authoritative, states clearly that Abraham offered his son Isaac on the altar on Mount Moriah (see Genesis 22:9–12). Islam claims that Ishmael was the son whom Abraham offered.

The direct opposition of the teaching of Mohammed to that of Jesus is mirrored at large in the contemporary world situation, and particularly in the Middle East. There is a single, spiritual force that unites the nations of the Middle East in fierce, unyielding opposition to the outworking of God's purposes for Israel: *It is Islam.*

It is fashionable to call the non-Jewish peoples of the Middle East "Arabs," but that actually is a misnomer. The Arabs are Semites—descendants of Shem, with Abraham as their ancestor. The nations of North Africa, on the other hand—such as Egypt, Libya, Tunisia, Morocco, Algeria and the Sudan—are for the most part descendants of Ham, not Shem. They have a completely different ancestry from that of true Arabs. Even the people of Iran, though they are Semites, are Persians, not Arabs. The inherent opposition of Mohammed's teaching to that of Jesus and the Bible finds its logical expression in the opposition of the Muslim nations to the people of Jesus (Israel) and to the outworking of God's purposes for Israel as revealed in the Bible. Thus, the conflict in the Middle East has its real origin in opposing spiritual forces, not in nationalistic or economic factors.

When history has run its course, however, the false revelation of Mohammed, and all that has come out of it, will be overthrown and stripped of all power and influence. Only what is built on the unshakable rock of Scripture will endure.

Isaiah 44:25 reveals yet another source of potential opposition to the prophetic revelation of Scripture. God not only "foils the signs of false prophets and makes fools of diviners"; He also "overthrows the learning of the wise and turns it into nonsense." Let me give a specific example of this, which I came across a good many years ago.

The *Encyclopedia Britannica* probably contains as much of the "learning of the wise" as any book published today. In the edition published in 1911, I once came across an article by a learned German professor concerning the pronunciation of ancient Hebrew. I cannot quote the passage verbatim, but the essence of what the professor said was as follows:

> The possibility that we can ever again recover the correct pronunciation of ancient Hebrew is as remote as the possibility that a Jewish Empire will ever again be established in the Middle East.

Thirty-seven years later, in 1948, the event the professor had dismissed as impossible took place. The learning of that wise professor was made foolish. Why? Because what he said opposed the predictions of God's prophets in Scripture, which predictions must stand and be fulfilled.

In Isaiah 46, God again affirms that His control over the affairs of the universe is absolute and that His prophetic Word determines the course of history:

> "Remember the former things, those of long ago;
>   I am God, and there is no other;
>   I am God, and there is none like me.
> I make known the end from the beginning,
>   from ancient times, what is still to come.
> I say: My purpose will stand,
>   and I will do all that I please."

verses 9–10

We must bear in mind that it is almighty God who is speaking. He it is who makes known the end from the beginning. His purpose will stand, and He will do all He pleases. The question is not whether God's Word will be fulfilled, but how we will relate ourselves to the outworking of that Word in the history and circumstances of our time.

5

THE PROCESS
OF REGATHERING

The prophetic Word of God reveals His predetermined purpose
to regather and restore Israel, as we have seen in the previous
chapter. God's Word does not confine itself, however, to the
mere revelation of His purpose. It also unfolds, with characteristic
vividness, the process by which that purpose will be carried out. In
particular, the prophet Jeremiah provides us with a whole series of
word pictures illustrating the process of Israel's regathering.

In Jeremiah 16, the prophet proclaims what may aptly be called
"the second exodus," and his proclamation falls into two sections.
First, he declares that this second exodus will be so great that it will
completely overshadow the original exodus of Israel from Egypt
under Moses. Second, he describes vividly the kind of agents God
will use to bring about the second exodus.

The Second Exodus

First, Jeremiah contrasts the original exodus from Egypt with the second:

> "However, the days are coming," declares the LORD, "when men will no longer say, 'As surely as the LORD lives, who brought the Israelites up out of Egypt,' but they will say, 'As surely as the LORD lives, who brought the Israelites up out of the land of the north and out of all the countries where he had banished them.' For I will restore them to the land I gave their forefathers."
>
> Jeremiah 16:14–15

For anyone familiar with the history and culture of the Jewish people, this statement is truly amazing—especially coming from one of their own acknowledged major prophets. For more than 3,000 years, in their annual Passover festival, the Jewish people have celebrated their deliverance from Egypt as the single greatest event in their history.

Yet a day is coming, declares Jeremiah, when this great Passover deliverance will pale into insignificance by comparison with the second ingathering of the Jewish people from all lands—particularly from the land of the north, which includes Germany, Poland and Russia. The wonder of this second worldwide exodus will so far exceed that of the first out of Egypt! Like Isaiah, Jeremiah looks forward to events of a much greater order than the limited return of the Jews from Babylon under Zerubbabel. For my part, when I apply Jeremiah's words to the regathering of Israel taking place in this century and the last, I feel that his evaluation is already correct, even though this second exodus is still far from complete.

Certainly the first deliverance out of Egypt was accompanied by tremendous signs and awe-inspiring miracles. By contrast, it is more difficult to form a single, comprehensive picture of the present deliverance of the Jewish people out of all nations.

Yet when I consider all the different intertwining circumstances that make this second deliverance possible, and when I take into account the diverse and numerous crises in the past century in which God sovereignly intervened to bring His prophetic Word to fulfillment, I conclude that this second deliverance is already greater than the first. And the end is not yet!

Jeremiah 16:16 gives a vivid picture of the agents God will use to bring about this second deliverance of the Jewish people, especially from the lands of the north:

> "But now I will send for many fishermen," declares the LORD, "and they will catch them. After that I will send for many hunters, and they will hunt them down on every mountain and hill and from the crevices of the rocks."

It was my first wife, Lydia, now home with the Lord, who pointed out to me that this verse describes exactly what happened to the Jews in Europe before and during World War II. Keep in mind that a fisherman draws his prey toward him with bait, and a hunter drives his from behind by fear. This was the order of events in Europe—especially in Germany.

First, God sent the "fishermen" (the Zionists) from Palestine to Europe, with this message: "Escape while there is still time. The situation will get worse, not better." Those who heeded this message left while they could. When the fishermen had finished their task, God sent the hunters.

We have to acknowledge that there are times when God is capable of a certain ruthlessness. If He has once set His mind to do a certain thing, then He will use whatever means are necessary to achieve His purpose. In this case, the Nazis were the hunters.

In 1966, I was preaching in West Berlin on the Bible's picture of the close of the present age. I was speaking in a large public auditorium to a gathering of about five hundred Germans. By way of illustration, I listed significant events or trends that, taken together, would indicate that the close of the age was at hand. One event I mentioned was the regathering of Israel in their own land.

At this point in my message, I referred to the verse quoted above— Jeremiah 16:16. As my interpreter read out the verse in German, a language I understand, I suddenly realized I was speaking to the very people from whose midst the "hunters" had been drawn. How was I to point out the exact fulfillment of the verse in recent history, without unnecessarily offending my hearers?

My whole audience grew unnaturally silent, uneasy with the direction my message was taking. For a moment I paused, searching for the right words. Then I said simply, "With your own eyes you have witnessed the fulfillment of this verse. Better than any others, you know how true these words are."

I did not need to say any more. No one could deny what I had said. So accurate is God's Word, and so relevant to our time!

In the Potter's Hand

In Jeremiah 18, the prophet presents another vivid picture of the process God will use to work out His end-time purposes for Israel. This time, God declares that He Himself will play the part of a potter:

> This is the word that came to Jeremiah from the LORD: "Go down to the potter's house, and there I will give you my message." So I went down to the potter's house, and I saw him working at the wheel. But the pot he was shaping from the clay was marred in his hands; so the potter formed it into another pot, shaping it as seemed best to him.
> Then the word of the LORD came to me: "O house of Israel, can I not do with you as this potter does?" declares the LORD. "Like clay in the hand of the potter, so are you in my hand, O house of Israel."
>
> Jeremiah 18:1–6

Have you ever seen a potter fashioning a pot on his wheel? There are various places in Israel today where you may see this.

I stood one day and watched a potter as he worked the clay in his hands. He pumped the treadle with his feet, and the wheel spun around while he held the pot against the spinning wheel. As I watched the potter at work, I understood the principle: *He used the pressure from the spinning wheel to form the pot to the shape he desired.*

This scene brought to my mind the passage quoted above. Jeremiah does more here than state a general principle; he also makes a specific prediction. Israel is the pot, and the Lord is the potter. The first time the Lord set out to make Israel His people, the pot was marred in His hand. Nevertheless, He did not cast it away. Instead He said, "I will make you over again into another pot, as it seems best to Me."

This is what is happening today. The Lord is using with Israel the same principle as the potter with the clay—the principle of applied pressure. Over the last three or four decades, Israel has been under continuous pressure: economic, military, psychological, political and spiritual (see special section). What is the meaning of all this? Nothing happens by accident. God is at work reshaping His people, as it seems best to Him.

Birth Pains of a New Age

Further on, Jeremiah returns to the theme of Israel's regathering:

This is the word that came to Jeremiah from the LORD: "This is what the LORD, the God of Israel, says: 'Write in a book all the words I have spoken to you. The days are coming,' declares the LORD, 'when I will bring my people Israel and Judah back from captivity and restore them to the land I gave their forefathers to possess,' says the LORD."

These are the words the LORD spoke concerning Israel and Judah: "This is what the LORD says:

"'Cries of fear are heard—
    terror, not peace.
Ask and see:
    Can a man bear children?
Then why do I see every strong man
    with his hands on his stomach like a woman in labor,
    every face turned deathly pale?
How awful that day will be!
    None will be like it.

It will be a time of trouble for Jacob,
but he will be saved out of it.'"

Jeremiah 30:1–7

God here charges Jeremiah to set down in permanent written form the prophecies He has given concerning Israel, that they may be available at the future time of their fulfillment. This is the very time, I believe, in which we are now living! Once more, God affirms His promise to regather Israel. At the same time, however, He warns that stability and peace will not come immediately. Rather, God speaks here of fear and terror and of a time of trouble without parallel in all the troubled history of Israel. So tremendous will be the pressures that even strong men will behave "like a woman in labor." All these things will constitute the "birth pains" that must usher in a new age of righteousness and peace.

In a parallel passage (Matthew 24:4–13), Jesus echoes this prophecy of Jeremiah. He, too, looks forward to a tumultuous period just prior to the close of the present age. He speaks of a great increase in international wars, famines and earthquakes. Then He adds the comment, "All these are the beginning of birth pains" (verse 8).

The prophecy of Jesus is wider in its scope, however, than that of Jeremiah. Whereas Jeremiah focuses on Israel and the Middle East, Jesus speaks of events and trends that will affect the *entire world*.

Continuing with the theme of Israel's restoration in the next chapter of Jeremiah, God Himself emphasizes the absolute, unalterable certainty of the mercy that He has promised His people:

> "The days are coming," declares the LORD, "when I will plant the house of Israel and the house of Judah with the offspring of men and of animals. Just as I watched over them to uproot and tear down, and to overthrow, destroy and bring disaster, so I will watch over them to build and to plant," declares the LORD.

Jeremiah 31:27–28

Before I became a Christian minister, when I was a professional philosopher, one of my favorite themes was logic. I have carried this respect for logic into my studies of Scripture, and I find the logic of the Bible more compelling than any work of human philosophy.

So it is with the passage quoted above—I see no way around its clear logic. The phrase *just as* at the beginning of verse 28 indicates an exact correspondence between two related acts of God toward Israel: on the one hand, the process of destruction and desolation; and on the other hand, the process of regathering and restoration.

God accepts personal responsibility for both. He declares that just as He watched over Israel and Judah to bring evil upon them, so He will now watch over them to do them good.

For me, the meaning of this is plain and inescapable. The same God who brought evil upon Israel will also be the One to bring good upon them. There cannot be any change in the identity of God. Likewise, there cannot be any change in the identity of Israel. The same people who received evil from the hand of God will be the ones to receive good from His hand. Nor is there any suggestion that the evil that came upon Israel was "literal" but that the good now promised will somehow be "metaphorical." Any such attempted interpretation of this passage violates the clear requirements of logic.

A New Covenant

We have already seen that the ultimate purpose of God's restoration of Israel is spiritual. Further on in Jeremiah, God declares that Israel broke the first covenant God made at the time He brought them out of Egypt, but that His spiritual purpose will be fulfilled when He initiates a new covenant with Israel at the time of their second regathering:

> "The time is coming," declares the LORD,
>   "when I will make a new covenant
> with the house of Israel
>   and with the house of Judah.
> It will not be like the covenant
>   I made with their forefathers

when I took them by the hand
    to lead them out of Egypt,
because they broke my covenant,
    though I was a husband to them,"
    declares the LORD.
"This is the covenant I will make with the house of Israel
    after that time," declares the LORD.
"I will put my law in their minds
    and write it on their hearts.
I will be their God,
    and they will be my people.
No longer will a man teach his neighbor,
    or a man his brother, saying, 'Know the LORD,'
because they will all know me,
    from the least of them to the greatest,"
    declares the LORD.
"For I will forgive their wickedness
    and will remember their sins no more."

Jeremiah 31:31–34

In Jeremiah 50, God makes further reference to this new covenant:

"In those days, at that time,"
    declares the LORD,
"the people of Israel and the people of Judah together
    will go in tears to seek the LORD their God.
They will ask the way to Zion
    and turn their faces toward it.
They will come and bind themselves to the LORD
    in an everlasting covenant
    that will not be forgotten."

Jeremiah 50:4–5

Here we see that as Israel and Judah "ask the way to Zion," they will be led into this new covenant relationship with the Lord. Unlike the covenant made at Sinai, this new covenant will be an everlasting one.

On the basis of this new and everlasting covenant, God also gives His personal guarantee, as stated in Jeremiah 31, that Israel will continue to exist forever as a distinct and recognized nation:

> This is what the LORD says,
>
> he who appoints the sun
>   to shine by day,
> who decrees the moon and stars
>   to shine by night,
> who stirs up the sea
>   so that its waves roar—
> the LORD Almighty is his name:
> "Only if these decrees vanish from my sight,"
>   declares the LORD,
> "will the descendants of Israel ever cease
>   to be a nation before me."
>
> verses 35–36

The terms of the guarantee are clear: As long as the sun, moon and stars continue in their courses, so long will Israel continue as a nation.

In Jeremiah 33, God again emphasizes that the ultimate purpose of restoration is not merely geographical or political, but spiritual:

> "I will bring Judah and Israel back from captivity and will rebuild them as they were before. I will cleanse them from all the sin they have committed against me and will forgive all their sins of rebellion against me."
>
> verses 7–8

Through repentance and forgiveness, Israel will finally and forever be reconciled to the Lord and restored to His favor. All that is now taking place is preparation for this glorious climax. The prophetic Word of God is unequivocal in its exposure and reproof of Israel's sins. At the same time, however, it contains repeated warnings against concluding that God has finally rejected Israel as a people. Further on in Jeremiah 33, the Lord specifically rules out any such conclusion:

The word of the LORD came to Jeremiah: "Have you not noticed that these people are saying, 'The LORD has rejected the two kingdoms he chose'? So they despise my people and no longer regard them as a nation. This is what the LORD says: 'If I have not established my covenant with day and night and the fixed laws of heaven and earth, then I will reject the descendants of Jacob and David my servant and will not choose one of his sons to rule over the descendants of Abraham, Isaac and Jacob. For I will restore their fortunes and have compassion on them.'"

verses 23–26

In these verses, God puts His finger on a certain attitude toward Israel that is expressed in the words, "The LORD has rejected the two kingdoms he chose"—meaning Israel and Judah. God says that those who hold and propagate this view of Israel are guilty of "despising" His people, because they no longer regard them as a nation. Unfortunately, this view of Israel has found expression in various forms of Christian theology for centuries and is still held by some Christians today.

God rejects this theology emphatically. He still regards Israel as His people and restates His commitment to restore them both to their land and to His favor.

The End Purpose: God's Glory

Ezekiel, the next major prophet after Jeremiah, also dwells at length on Israel's restoration. Chapter 36 of his prophecy is devoted to this theme, revealing the great underlying purpose that prompts God's promise of restoration:

"Therefore say to the house of Israel, 'This is what the Sovereign LORD says: It is not for your sake, O house of Israel, that I am going to do these things, but for the sake of my holy name, which you have profaned among the nations where you have gone. I will show the holiness of my great name, which has been profaned among the nations, the name you have profaned among them. Then the nations will know that I am the LORD, declares the Sovereign LORD, when I show myself holy through you before their eyes.'"

verses 22–23

We must grasp one clear fact about Israel's restoration: God does not commit Himself to restore Israel because they deserve it. On the contrary, He makes it clear that they do not. Restoration is promised on the basis of God's grace and mercy. Through Israel's restoration, God will restore to His own name the glory that has so long been tarnished by Israel's misdeeds. In fact, God's glory is the only final and sufficient purpose for anything He does.

At the same time, God is also committed to the spiritual restoration of the Church, although the Church does not deserve restoration any more than Israel does. If we examine the parallel histories of Israel and the Church over the past eighteen centuries, it would be hard to say which has failed God more grievously. In each case, restoration springs from God's grace and mercy, not from human deserts. And, in each case, the end purpose is God's glory.

Christians have little difficulty seeing that the Jewish people do not deserve God's mercy. They might be surprised, however, to learn how clearly the Jewish people, for their part, see that the Church does not deserve God's mercy. In neither case is it a question of deserts, but only of God's sovereign choice and unmerited favor.

Having first stated His purpose, God then reveals the steps by which He will carry out that purpose:

> "For I will take you out of the nations; I will gather you from all the countries and bring you back into your own land. I will sprinkle clean water on you, and you will be clean; I will cleanse you from all your impurities and from all your idols."

verses 24–25

These verses confirm what we have already seen. The first part of restoration is political, but the end purpose is spiritual—cleansing from all impurity. It seems to be a principle of God's Word that there is only one place on earth where He will deal with Israel as a nation, and this is in their own land.

This principle is stated more specifically in Hosea, in which the "place" referred to is the land of Israel:

> "Yet the Israelites will be like the sand on the seashore, which cannot be measured or counted. In the place where it was said to them, 'You are not my people,' they will be called 'sons of the living God.'"

Hosea 1:10

A New Heart and Spirit

Ezekiel next reveals a vital turning point in this transition from the natural and political to the spiritual: "I will give you a new heart and put a new spirit in you; I will remove from you your heart of stone and give you a heart of flesh" (Ezekiel 36:26).

This verse seems to describe just what God is doing at the present time. He is in the process of taking from the Jewish people their heart of stone and giving them back a heart of flesh.

I have been in personal, ongoing contact with Israel and with the Jewish people since 1942, when I first visited Jerusalem. To mention only one aspect, my second wife, Ruth, and I number among the adopted children in our combined family nine who are Jewish.

The period from 1942 to 2002 represents a little more than a biblical generation. In this generation, a significant change has taken place in the general attitude of the Jewish people toward the work of the Holy Spirit and toward the Person of Jesus.

If I were asked to name one date that was central to this change, I would point to 1967, the year of the Six-Day War, when the Jewish people once again regained political control over the Old City of Jerusalem (see special section, p. 150). From that time onward, the Jewish people have displayed a new warmth and openness toward the Person of Jesus. For the first time in many centuries, they are beginning to claim Him as one of their own. New books about Him by Jewish authors are appearing continually in Israel. A corresponding attitude of warmth and openness also extends today toward Christians who love the Jewish people with sincerity and God's own unchanging love for them.

The condition of a "heart of stone" came upon the Jewish people as a judgment from God for their persistent stubbornness and for their refusal to hear His voice and heed His prophets. Only God Himself can reverse this judgment and restore to them a heart of flesh. In His mercy and wisdom, He set a predetermined time to do this—a time here predicted by the prophet Ezekiel. It is now happening before our eyes!

The Jewish people are once again ready to receive and respond to God's Holy Spirit. Ezekiel also predicts this next stage of restoration: "And I will put my Spirit in you and move you to follow my decrees and be careful to keep my laws" (Ezekiel 36:27).

One important revelation, which runs through the entire Bible, is that we can never obey God's laws merely by our own strength or willpower. Only one power can enable us to do this—the power of the Holy Spirit.

This is implicit in the order of the promises that God here gives to Israel. First He will restore His Holy Spirit to them; then He will move them to keep His decrees and laws. I believe that perhaps the greatest mistake the Jewish people have made through the centuries is trying to keep God's laws merely in the strength of their own natural willpower. Many professing Christians have made the same mistake. The truth is, nobody can do this, whether he is Jew or Christian.

This lesson has been made vivid for me through my own personal experience. I was born and brought up in the Anglican Church of Britain. At fifteen, as a scholar at Eton College, I was confirmed in the college chapel. At the close of that ceremony, I determined that from then on I was going to be better than I ever had been before.

But what happened? Instead of getting better, I got progressively worse. For about six months, I struggled with my problem, but in vain. Then I said to myself, "This doesn't work—at least, not for me." The root of my problem was that I was trying to obey God and do His will without the power of the Holy Spirit.

Then, about ten years later, during World War II, I received a supernatural infilling of the Holy Spirit. This experience so changed my inner desires, attitudes and values that from then on doing the will of God was no longer a struggle but a delight. It was the power of the Holy Spirit within me that brought about this change.

On the basis of my own experience, therefore, I find it easy to believe this promise of God in Ezekiel 36:27—that He will once again put His Holy Spirit within the Jewish people and so bring them back into true and full obedience to His laws and decrees. No Jew waits more eagerly than I do for the fulfillment of this promise to Israel!

On the basis of this new obedience, inspired and empowered by the Holy Spirit, God promises Israel full and permanent restoration in their relationship with God Himself: "You will live in the land I gave your forefathers; you will be my people, and I will be your God" (Ezekiel 36:28).

Once again, the order of the promises given in this verse is important. The ultimate is not living in the land, but rather the restored relationship to God.

A Glimpse of Dawn

For a final summary of God's promised restoration of Israel, we turn to the prophet Amos. Of all the Hebrew prophets, none was more emphatic than Amos in his denunciation of Israel's many sins or more severe in his warning of the impending judgments. Indeed, this is the main theme that runs throughout the nine chapters of the book of Amos.

But in the last few verses of the entire book, there is a dramatic transition from warnings of judgment to promises of mercy. Reading through Amos is like passing through a long, tempestuous night and then at the end catching a brief glimpse of a serene and radiant dawn.

Let us consider those two closing verses:

"I will bring back my exiled people Israel;
   they will rebuild the ruined cities and live in them.
They will plant vineyards and drink their wine;

> they will make gardens and eat their fruit.
> I will plant Israel in their own land,
>   never again to be uprooted
> from the land I have given them,"
>   says the LORD your God.

Amos 9:14–15

Verse 14 contains four successive predictions, each of which is being fulfilled before our eyes.

First, "I will bring back my exiled people Israel," which we have discussed at length.

Second, "They will rebuild the ruined cities and live in them." Upon returning to their land, the Jewish people have taken special pleasure in locating the sites of ancient cities mentioned in the Bible and building modern cities there. Some examples are: Arad (see Numbers 21:1); Beer Sheba (see Genesis 21:31); Giloh (see 2 Samuel 15:12); and four cities that belonged originally to the Philistines: Ashkelon, Ashdod, Gath (see 1 Samuel 6:17) and Beth Shean (see 1 Samuel 31:10–12).

Third, "They will plant vineyards and drink their wine." Since the regathering of Israel, many vineyards have been planted in various areas of the country. In the time of the Maccabees, Israel was famous for its wine. The restored industry of viniculture is once again flourishing.

Fourth, "They will make gardens and eat their fruit." If ever there were a garden-loving people, it is the people of modern Israel. Both the cities and the countryside abound with newly planted gardens. The people of Israel enjoy in abundance the fruit of these gardens, and they also export the fruit to many other nations.

At one time, the "experts" predicted cynically that "the Jews will never succeed with their agriculture. They know nothing about farming. All they know about is money." It is amusing to note that today, over fifty years later, Israel is recognized as one of the most successful agricultural nations in the world, whereas its economy has run into almost ceaseless problems. So much for the predictions of the experts!

In light of the fulfillment of the four specific predictions contained in Amos 9:14, we can look forward with faith to the fulfillment of God's final, comprehensive promise to Israel in the following verse:

> "I will plant Israel in their own land,
> never again to be uprooted
> from the land I have given them,"
> says the LORD your God.
>
> verse 15

There are three important points to note in this verse. First, God calls the land to which He restores Israel "their own land." Second, God promises that their restoration this time will be permanent; they will "never again be uprooted." Third, God speaks of the land "I *have* given them." The giving of the land to Israel is already settled in the eternal counsels of God.

Twice in past history, the people of Israel have entered and settled in the land—the first time as conquerors led by Joshua; the second time as exiles returning from Babylon under Zerubbabel. In each case, however, after occupying the land for some time, they were uprooted and driven out. Thus, no previous occupation fulfilled the promise given in Amos 9:15. We are left, then, with only two possible conclusions: Either there is still to be a permanent occupation of the land by Israel; or else the Bible is not a reliable book. For my part, I believe Israel is now receiving permanent possession of the land, just as God here promises: "never again to be uprooted."

6

THE TIMES OF
THE GENTILES

U p to this point, all the prophecies that we have examined concerning Israel's restoration have been taken from the Old Testament. Our overview would be incomplete, however, without taking into account the teaching of the New Testament. The Bible's long line of Hebrew prophets culminates with Jesus. What does He have to say on the theme of Israel's restoration?

The answer is found primarily in the great prophetic discourse that Jesus gave on the Mount of Olives, just before His arrest, trial and death. This discourse is recorded in all three of the synoptic gospels—in Matthew 24, Mark 13 and Luke 21. Each writer brings out certain features of the discourse not brought out by the others. In order to form a comprehensive picture of all that Jesus predicts, therefore, it is necessary to set the three versions side by side. Luke's version is the one that relates most directly to Israel's dispersal and restoration, so we will focus mainly on it.

The discourse arose out of a statement Jesus made about the buildings of the Temple: "As for what you see here, the time will come when not one stone will be left on another; every one of them will be thrown down" (Luke 21:6). Later, when Jesus was with His disciples on the Mount of Olives, directly overlooking the Temple buildings, the disciples reverted to His statement and asked, "When will these things happen? And what will be the sign that they are about to take place?" (Luke 21:7).

Matthew records a further question posed by the disciples: "And what will be the sign of your coming and of the end of the age?" (Matthew 24:3).

The disciples imagined that their two questions referred to the same period. They assumed that the destruction of the Temple would also mark the end of the age. Our own perspective, looking back over 2,000 years of history, is different. We realize that the destruction of the Temple occurred in AD 70 but that the end of the age has not yet come.

Signs of the End

Jesus's reply, as recorded in Luke 21, deals first, briefly, with their question about the end of the age. He begins with a negative approach, warning them of certain things that will occur but that will *not* necessarily point to the end of the age:

> He replied, "Watch out that you are not deceived. For many will come in my name, claiming, 'I am he,' and, 'The time is near.' Do not follow them. When you hear of wars and revolutions, do not be frightened. These things must happen first, but the end will not come right away."
>
> Luke 21:8–9

Here, then, are two kinds of events that do *not* necessarily indicate that the end of the age is near: first, the coming of many false messiahs; and second, reports of wars and revolutions. The words of Jesus have proven true. Jewish history records more than forty false messiahs since the time Jesus was on earth. (Sabbatai Zevi, mentioned in chapter 2, is one example.) World history likewise records countless wars and revolutions. Yet the age has not come to an end.

In the next verses, Jesus addresses the disciples' question from a positive standpoint. He speaks of five kinds of events that *will* point to the end of the age:

> Then he said to them: "Nation will rise against nation, and kingdom against kingdom. There will be great earthquakes, famines and pestilences in various places, and fearful events and great signs from heaven."
>
> verses 10–11

Here, then, are five kinds of events that, when they occur together and with increasing frequency, *will* indicate that the end of the age is near: first, great international wars; second, great earthquakes; third, famines; fourth, pestilences; fifth, fearful and unusual phenomena in the heavens.

Jesus then commences a new section of His discourse with the words, "But before all this . . ." In verses 8 through 11, He has been looking ahead to the events leading up to the end of the age. But in verse 12, He returns to the situation in His own day. There on the Mount of Olives, He warns the disciples of events and experiences they must be prepared to face in their own generation:

> "But before all this, they will lay hands on you and persecute you. They will deliver you to synagogues and prisons, and you will be brought before kings and governors, and all on account of my name. This will result in your being witnesses to them. But make up your mind not to worry beforehand how you will defend yourselves. For I will give you words and wisdom that none of your adversaries will be able to resist or contradict. You will be betrayed even by parents, brothers, relatives and friends, and they will put some of you to death. All men will hate you because of me. But not a hair of your head will perish. By standing firm you will gain life."
>
> verses 12–19

Everything Jesus predicts here actually happened to the disciples in the first century. Confirmation is found in the New Testament itself—in the book of Acts and on through to the opening chapters of the book of Revelation.

The Destruction of the Temple

In the next section, Jesus answers the disciples' question, which originally provoked His discourse, about the destruction of the Temple. He focuses on three related topics: the city of Jerusalem, the land of Israel and the destiny of the Jewish people.

> "When you see Jerusalem being surrounded by armies, you will know that its desolation is near. Then let those who are in Judea flee to the mountains, let those in the city get out, and let those in the country not enter the city. For this is the time of punishment in fulfillment of all that has been written. How dreadful it will be in those days for pregnant women and nursing mothers!"
>
> verses 20–23

Jesus reveals the key event that will signal the impending destruction of the Temple and of the whole city of Jerusalem: "When you see *Jerusalem being surrounded by armies*, you will know that its desolation is near" (emphasis added). Any of His disciples who might at that time be in Jerusalem or in the surrounding countryside, or anywhere in Judea, are told to flee.

History confirms the pinpoint accuracy of Jesus's prophetic warning. In AD 70, the Roman legions advanced against Jerusalem to lay siege to it, then raised the siege temporarily and withdrew. Those Jews in Jerusalem and in the surrounding countryside who were disciples of Jesus recognized this as the sign of impending destruction. Obeying His instruction, they fled to the city of Pella outside Judea, thus saving their lives. Shortly afterward, the Roman legions again laid siege to Jerusalem and continued until they had destroyed the entire city, including the Temple.

In verse 22, Jesus says that, for the Jewish people, this would be "the time of punishment in fulfillment of all that has been written" and that the suffering would particularly affect pregnant women and nursing mothers.

The phrase *all that has been written* refers to the warnings given to the Jewish people by their own prophets in the Old Testament. One of the most vivid—and the most terrible—is found in Deuteronomy:

> The LORD will bring a nation against you from far away . . . a fierce-looking nation without respect for the old or pity for the young. They will devour the young of your livestock and the crops of your land until you are destroyed. They will leave you no grain, new wine or oil, nor any calves of your herds or lambs of your flocks until you are ruined. They will lay siege to all the cities throughout your land until the high fortified walls in which you trust fall down. They will besiege all the cities throughout the land the LORD your God is giving you.
>
> Because of the suffering that your enemy will inflict on you during the siege, *you will eat the fruit of the womb, the flesh of the sons and daughters the LORD your God has given you.* . . . The most gentle and sensitive woman among you . . . will begrudge the husband she loves and her own son or daughter the afterbirth from her womb and the children she bears. *For she intends to eat them secretly during the siege* and in the distress that your enemy will inflict on you in your cities.
>
> Deuteronomy 28:49–57, emphasis added

All these things predicted by Moses did, in fact, happen to the Jewish people during the Roman invasion and the siege of Jerusalem. They are recorded in detail by the Jewish historian Josephus Flavius. It is significant that Moses, like Jesus, laid special emphasis on the ordeal that the siege would impose on pregnant women and nursing mothers.

Josephus relates one particularly terrible incident during the siege of Jerusalem that strikingly confirms the accuracy of the predictions of both Moses and Jesus. Mary, the daughter of Eleazar—a Jewish woman from a wealthy family—became so desperate with hunger that she killed her nursing infant son, roasted his flesh and ate half of it.

Attracted by the smell of roasting flesh, a group of Jewish fighters burst in on her, intending to take her food for themselves. But when the woman defiantly exposed the half-eaten body of her son and invited them to help themselves, even these hardened fighters recoiled in revulsion and left the woman to finish off her unnatural food by herself.

Times of Distress

"There will be great distress in the land and wrath against this people. They will fall by the sword and will be taken as prisoners to all the nations. Jerusalem will be trampled on by the Gentiles until the times of the Gentiles are fulfilled."

Luke 21:23–24

Here Jesus is depicting the results of the Roman invasion: "great distress in the land and wrath against this people." As predicted, the Jewish people "fell by the sword"—more than 1 million of them. Nearly 100,000 others were captured, sold in the slave markets of Rome and "taken as prisoners to all the nations."

On occasion, Bible prophecy covers a long period of time with a single brief phrase or sentence. In such cases, the purpose is to emphasize an important spiritual connection between two events, even though these may be separated widely in time.

The latter part of Luke 21:24 is a good example of this: "Jerusalem will be trampled on by the Gentiles." This prediction spans at least nineteen centuries. It commenced with the capture of Jerusalem by the Roman armies. Its fulfillment brings us close once more to "the end of the age."

The three verses that immediately follow close with the actual "coming of the Son of Man"—that is, the visible return of Jesus in glory:

"There will be signs in the sun, moon and stars. On the earth, nations will be in anguish and perplexity at the roaring and tossing of the sea. Men will faint from terror, apprehensive of what is coming on the world, for the heavenly bodies will be shaken. At that time they will see the Son of Man coming in a cloud with power and great glory."

verses 25–27

As we summed up briefly the predictions of Jesus concerning Jerusalem, the Jewish people and their land, the following order of events emerged:

1. The destruction of the Temple and of the city of Jerusalem.
2. A long period called "the times of the Gentiles," during which Jerusalem will be under the domination of Gentile powers.
3. A brief period of worldwide upheaval and distress, culminating in the "coming of the Son of Man."

Further, Jesus reveals that the end of the "times of the Gentiles" will be signaled by a change in the status of Jerusalem. What will be the nature of that change?

The Government of Jerusalem

In Luke 21:24, Jesus speaks of Jerusalem as being "trampled on by the Gentiles." This phrase implies that it is, in some deep sense, wrong or unnatural for a Gentile power to have dominion over Jerusalem. From the time of David onward, God committed the responsibility for caring for this unique city to the Jewish people. The only reason it has ever passed into other hands is that, through disobedience toward God, the Jewish people have forfeited their God-given privilege.

This interpretation is confirmed by the record of history. Under Jewish government, the city has always grown and flourished. Under Gentile government, by contrast, it has usually languished.

It is clear, then, that "the times of the Gentiles" refers to the period of Jerusalem's history during which it is governed by Gentile powers. The word translated "Gentiles" means, literally, "nations" and reflects accurately the city's subsequent history. After capture by Rome, Jerusalem was ruled by at least ten other Gentile nations in the next eighteen centuries—among these the Byzantine Empire, the Persians, the Arabs, the Crusaders, the Ottoman Empire, the British and the Jordanians.

In Jesus's prediction, however, one key word indicates a limit to the period of Gentile domination—the word *until*. Jerusalem will indeed be trampled on by the Gentiles, but not forever; only until "the times of the Gentiles are fulfilled." This means that the end of the times of the Gentiles will be marked by a specific event: *The government of Jerusalem will once again pass into the hands of the Jewish people.*

Can we say that this event has taken place?

Before answering that question, we need to define the area Jesus referred to as "Jerusalem." First and foremost, it contained the Temple area. Second, it contained most, although not all, of the area to the west and north of the Temple, which is now enclosed within the walls of the Old City. Third, it included an area to the west and south of the Temple that is not contained within the present walls of the Old City. This third area contained what is now called "Mount Zion" and also the hill that slopes southward from the Temple area to the Pool of Siloam, which archaeologists have identified as the "city of David."

Having defined the area, we can address our question: Who now exercises governmental control over this area? The answer is not in doubt: It is the Jewish people.

At what point did the control of this area pass out of Gentile hands and back into Jewish hands? Again, the answer is not in doubt: It was in June 1967, as a result of the Six-Day War (see special section, p. 150).

There is a distinction, of course, between *governmental* control and *absolute* control. The state of Israel now governs this whole area, but it does not exercise absolute control over it. The most sacred and controversial section—the actual area of the Temple—is still the site of a Muslim mosque in the hands of Arabs.

Nevertheless, when all due allowance has been made for the limits that are still set to Jewish sovereignty, the fact remains that in June 1967, the governmental control of Jerusalem as Jesus knew it passed out of Gentile hands and into Jewish hands.

It would be premature to say that this marked the end of "the times of the Gentiles." We could say, however, that it marked the *beginning of the end* of those times. It has been my privilege to live through what I consider to be the two most significant fulfillments of biblical prophecy since the first century. The first was the rebirth of the state of Israel in May 1948. The second was the reestablishment of Jewish government over the area that Jesus knew as Jerusalem in June 1967.

From Heaven's Viewpoint

Up to this point, we have been looking at the process of Israel's restoration only on a horizontal plane, from a human viewpoint. I would now like to relate some experiences of a friend that I believe will provide insight into how God views this whole process.

My friend, whom I will call "Pastor W," is an internationally recognized Bible teacher of proven integrity and maturity.

Sometime in the late '50s or early '60s, Pastor W was taking part in a home prayer meeting, when he was granted a vision of a scene in heaven. He saw a great throng of angels with their faces turned toward the earth. They were eagerly following events taking place on earth, and they obviously desired to participate in them. But a golden cord stretched in front of the angels held them back in their place in heaven. Pastor W was left wondering what this vision might mean.

Some years later, in another prayer meeting, he had a similar vision of the angels in heaven with the golden cord holding them back. This time, however, while Pastor W watched, the golden cord was drawn aside. Immediately, with obvious joy and excitement, the whole throng of angels descended to earth. Then the vision ended, and Pastor W was not able to see what the angels proceeded to do on earth.

Pastor W concluded that a sovereign angelic visitation was about to take place, and he began to tell his Christian friends to expect some tremendous work of the Holy Spirit in the area in which he had received the two visions.

Time passed, however, and nothing of special significance happened. Pastor W was disappointed and nonplussed, although he could not doubt the authenticity of his two visions.

After a considerable lapse of time, it occurred to him to check back over major world events that had occurred around the time of his second vision—the one in which the angels had been released to participate in the affairs of earth. Perhaps the vision was associated with some development in the world situation that was particularly significant from heaven's viewpoint. He quickly made a discovery that left no doubt as to the meaning of his second vision: *The day he received that vision was the first day of the Six-Day War.*

When Pastor W shared this vision with me, it made a profound impact. It confirmed what I had already inferred from my study of biblical prophecy and, in particular, from the words of Jesus in Luke 21:24.

The Six-Day War was an epoch—a decisive turning point in human history. The reestablishment of Jewish government over the area Jesus knew as Jerusalem marked a transition from one era to another. The era that Jesus called "the times of the Gentiles" is drawing to a close. In its place, a new era is dawning—an era that will usher in the government of God on earth, for Israel and for all nations.

In closing this section, let me share two thoughts relating to the words of Jesus in Luke 21:24 and also to the vision of my friend.

First, if the angels in heaven are so excited about the restoration of Jerusalem, ought not God's people on earth to be at least equally excited?

Second, if Jewish control of Jerusalem is essential to the establishment of God's Kingdom on earth, it explains the passionate opposition that this prospect provokes in so many political and religious circles. Satan realizes that his kingdom is being threatened as never before, and he is fighting back with every weapon and tactic he can muster.

It is vital that God's people do not succumb to Satan's tactics. We need to see the issues in the light of Scripture and not accept the warped view presented by the world's news media. Once we have seen the issues, we are obligated to take a firm, unflinching stand on the side of God's purposes and His people.

7

WHOSE IS THE LAND?

We must now face one of the most controversial issues in modern politics. It centers on a relatively small area of the earth's surface that, at various times in its history, has been known as the land of Canaan, the land of Israel, the Holy Land and Palestine. Part of this area is occupied currently by the modern state of Israel; the remainder is occupied by four surrounding Arab nations: Lebanon, Syria, Jordan and Egypt.

These Arab nations, together with other Arab nations in the Middle East, have been generally hostile to Israel. They have rejected Israel's claim to that part of the land it currently occupies; and, even more emphatically, they have rejected any claim to the whole area designated originally as the land of Israel.

Israel and these other nations continue to make claims and counterclaims, expressing different points of view and based on different periods of the land's history. I doubt whether any human court in existence today could pronounce a final, authoritative settlement of all these claims, acceptable to all the parties involved.

In view of this, I will appeal to a higher authority: the Bible. For those who accept the authority of the Bible, the ownership of the land is settled clearly and unambiguously.

One verse of Scripture declares the final, inalienable ownership of this land, as well as all other lands: "The earth is the LORD's, and everything in it, the world, and all who live in it" (Psalm 24:1).

By right of creation, God owns the entire earth and everything in it. The disposition God makes of any part of the earth, therefore, is sufficient to settle its ownership. Out of the whole earth, there is one particular area to which God lays special claim: the land of Israel.

In several passages of Scripture, God calls this "my land." Let us look at just two of these passages, both of which refer to situations in which Gentile nations are planning something in relation to the land and its people that is contrary to the will of God.

First, Ezekiel's prophecy looks toward an invasion of Israel by the northern confederacy of Gog and Magog at the close of this age. God Himself is speaking:

> "You will advance against *my people* Israel like a cloud that covers the land. In days to come, O Gog, I will bring you against *my land*, so that the nations may know me when I show myself holy through you before their eyes."
>
> Ezekiel 38:16, emphasis added

The second passage is found in the prophet Joel. Again, God is speaking:

> "I will gather all nations
>   and bring them down to the Valley of Jehoshaphat.
> There I will enter into judgment against them
>   concerning *my inheritance, my people Israel,*
> for they scattered *my people* among the nations
>   and divided up *my land.*"
>
> Joel 3:2, emphasis added

Three times in these passages God calls Israel "my people," and twice He calls their land "my land." We see, therefore, that God lays special claim to the land of Israel. He is most emphatic about this claim when the integrity of the land is challenged by Gentile nations.

An Everlasting Covenant

As absolute owner of this land, God has by His sovereign choice given it to a specific group of people—that is, to Abraham and his descendants. In Genesis, God reveals this sovereign decision to Abraham:

> "I will establish my covenant as an everlasting covenant between me and you and your descendants after you for the generations to come, to be your God and the God of your descendants after you. The whole land of Canaan, where you are now an alien, I will give as an everlasting possession to you and your descendants after you; and I will be their God."
>
> Genesis 17:7–8

The language here is emphatic and unambiguous: The *whole* land is given as an *everlasting* possession to Abraham and to his descendants after him. Thereafter, in the unfolding history of the book of Genesis, the land is given to Abraham's descendants—specifically, Isaac and Jacob.

God's promise to Isaac is found in chapter 26:

> "Stay in this land for a while, and I will be with you and will bless you. For to you and your descendants I will give all these lands and will confirm the oath I swore to your father Abraham. I will make your descendants as numerous as the stars in the sky and will give them all these lands, and through your offspring all nations on earth will be blessed."
>
> verses 3–4

Twice in these verses God uses the phrase *all these lands*. The plural form includes all the various areas that together make up the complete inheritance.

God's further promise of the land to Jacob is found in chapter 35:

And God said to him, "I am God Almighty; be fruitful and increase in number. A nation and a community of nations will come from you, and kings will come from your body. The land I gave to Abraham and Isaac I also give to you, and I will give this land to your descendants after you."

verses 11–12

When we put these three passages of Genesis together, the line of descent through which the land is promised is explicit. It was promised first to Abraham, then to Isaac, then to Jacob and then to Jacob's descendants after him. The collective name given to the nation descended from Jacob is, of course, *Israel*.

This revelation concerning the land of Canaan, or Israel, is summed up in one short passage in Psalm 105. The psalmist introduces the passage by stating that God enforces His judgments—that is, the sovereign determination of His will—in every part of the earth: "He is the LORD our God; his judgments are in all the earth" (verse 7).

From this introductory statement, the psalmist goes on to proclaim the specific judgments, or determinations, of God concerning the land of Canaan:

> He remembers his covenant forever,
> the word he commanded, for a thousand generations,
> the covenant he made with Abraham,
> the oath he swore to Isaac.
> He confirmed it to Jacob as a decree,
> to Israel as an everlasting covenant:
> "To you I will give the land of Canaan
> as the portion you will inherit."

verses 8–11

The psalmist emphasizes two important points. First, he leaves no doubt as to the line of descent through which the promise of the land is given. It is from Abraham, to Isaac, to Jacob, to Israel. Second, the psalmist uses every conceivable scriptural term to establish the sacred, unchanging nature of God's commitment to Abraham and his descendants. He speaks of God's own "covenant" and of "the word he commanded" and of "the oath he swore." Then he speaks of "a decree" and finally of "an everlasting covenant."

What a powerful list of words denoting God's unchanging commitment: *covenant, word, command, oath, decree* and, finally, *everlasting covenant*! I know of no other passage where Scripture speaks with greater or more sustained emphasis than this. And all this emphasis centers on one issue: the ownership of the land of Canaan.

Apart from Psalm 105, it is the prophetic passages predicting Israel's end-time restoration that stress most frequently Israel's ownership of the land. In other words, the Bible's emphasis on their right to the land does not diminish, but actually increases, with the passage of time. Some of the prophetic passages we have already examined confirm this:

> "The days are coming," declares the LORD, "when I will bring my people Israel and Judah back from captivity and restore them to the land I gave their forefathers to possess," says the LORD.
>
> Jeremiah 30:3

God speaks first of "my people Israel and Judah," then of "the land I gave their forefathers to possess." Only one land answers this description.

Next, let us set beside each other two verses from Ezekiel 36:

> "Son of man, when the people of Israel were living in their own land, they defiled it by their conduct and their actions. Their conduct was like a woman's monthly uncleanness in my sight."
>
> verse 17

When Israel originally occupied the land before their first captivity, even though they defiled it, God still called it "their own land."

Further on He states, "For I will take you out of the nations; I will gather you from all the countries and bring you back into your own land" (verse 24). When God promises to bring Israel back to the land at the close of the age, He still calls it "your own land." In God's sight, the ownership of the land has never changed and never will. He gave it to Abraham and his descendants by an everlasting covenant.

Finally, let us turn again briefly to Amos.

> "I will plant Israel in their own land,
>   never again to be uprooted
>   from the land I have given them,"
>   says the LORD your God.
>
> Amos 9:15

Here again, God is speaking of Israel's end-time restoration in "their own land." Furthermore, He promises that they will never again be uprooted. This promise, given nearly three thousand years ago, is neither affected nor modified by the growing might of the Arab nations today nor by their determination to destroy Israel. On the contrary, the current multiplication of problems and the violent opposition to Israel shows us why God, in His foresight, took such pains to emphasize Israel's inalienable right to the land.

Israel and All Nations

Why does God in His Word speak so frequently, and with such emphasis, about the ownership of this relatively small land? First and foremost, because He is a covenant-keeping God, and He wants the whole world to know it.

I believe there is another important principle involved, however, which is stated by Moses in Deuteronomy:

> When the Most High gave the nations their inheritance,
>   when he divided all mankind,
> he set up boundaries for the peoples
>   according to the number of the sons of Israel.
>
> Deuteronomy 32:8

God has not left it to chance to determine where each nation shall dwell. He has an appointed dwelling place for each section of the human race.

When God allotted the appointed areas to the nations, what was His starting point? Moses here tells us: It was from the land He had allotted to Israel. First, He chose Israel's inheritance for them; then He allotted the inheritance of the other nations in relationship to that of Israel. The area allotted to Israel was based on the size of population that God intended them ultimately to attain.

In the New Testament, this revelation is confirmed by a remarkable statement made by the apostle Paul in his speech to the men of Athens:

> From one man he [God] made every nation of men, that they should inhabit the whole earth; and he determined the times set for them and the exact places where they should live.
>
> Acts 17:26

We see, then, that God has determined not only *where* the nations shall dwell, but also *when* they shall dwell there. It is around God's dealings with Israel, however, and the inheritance He has appointed for them, that His dealings with all other nations revolve. Israel is both starting point and center.

To bring out the implications of this, let me use a simple parable from daily life. Suppose I am putting on a three-piece suit with a vest. The vest has five buttons. In buttoning up the vest, I make a mistake so that the top button ends up in the second hole. What will be the result? Problems all the way down! Every other button will likewise end up in the wrong hole, and when I get to the bottom, there will be one button left over without any hole for it.

Now apply this simple illustration to the nations on earth. Israel is the first button. If Israel is not in the right "hole," then there will be something wrong with the situation of every other nation on earth.

This revelation of God's Word has a vital, practical application for people from all other nations. When we consider God's plan for Israel, we cannot stand aside, as citizens of other lands, and say, "Israel's fate does not concern us." The fact is, the well-being of every nation is at stake. Until Israel enters into its full inheritance, the other nations can never enjoy the blessings that God has in store for them also.

The restoration of Israel has been accompanied by tremendous turmoil and upheaval. In chapter 3, I related some of what my family and I endured in Jerusalem during the period that the state of Israel was being established. Many more suffered similar things—people who were not guilty of any particular wrongdoing. Suffering came to all who lived in Jerusalem at the time—Jews, Arabs and all the rest.

For my part, however, I view my family's sufferings in the light of God's purpose revealed in Scripture. I can look back now and see that, through it all, God was working in His infinite wisdom to bring Israel back into their right place and into right relationship with Himself.

All that God is doing in the Middle East has this end in view. Doubtless there will be more suffering and upheavals. In the midst of it all, however, God will continue to work out His eternal purpose, as revealed in His prophetic Word. This assurance offers peace in the midst of turmoil.

I am neither a Jew nor an Arab. Yet I cannot for this reason remain neutral or indifferent. Like all people everywhere, I must face up to this fact: God is at work in the earth and particularly in the Middle East, bringing about the fulfillment of His predetermined plan. Ultimately, the well-being of all other nations is bound up with the fulfillment of God's plan for Israel.

Identification with God's Will

Over the years, as I have prayed about the situation in the Middle East and meditated on it in light of God's Word, I have found comfort and direction from a brief statement in the New Testament: "The one who does the will of God abides forever" (1 John 2:17, NASB).

Here is a clear promise of total and permanent security. To avail ourselves of it, we need to take two steps. First, we must discover God's will as it is revealed in Scripture. Then, by a firm decision of our own will, we must align ourselves with His purposes, both in our individual lives and in the events of world history taking place around us.

As we thus identify ourselves with the will of God, our lives are imbued with the very nature of His will—its stability and irresistible strength. These qualities are not threatened by the disorder in the world around us or by the seeming disasters that shout at us from the world's news media. Nor can they be affected by the irresponsible utterances and actions of Arab politicians or even of Israel's own leaders.

One thing is sure: God will carry out His predetermined plan for all nations, as revealed in Scripture. Once we have been confronted with the revelation of God's will, the decision required of us does not vary according to our racial or religious background. Whether we are Jews or Arabs, Africans, Asians or Americans, we are all required to renounce any plans or preconceptions contrary to the will of God and then to find our appointed place in the outworking of God's plan. Of course, the details of His plan will vary for nations as they do for individuals. We are not all cast in the same role. God has a specific place and function for each nation, as we have seen. Peace and harmony can come to the earth only as nations bow to the sovereign determination of God. Then each nation will be free to find its appointed place and fulfill its appointed function.

The details of the plan vary, but the basic issue does not vary, either for individuals or for nations, and it is this: submission to the revealed purposes of God. Here we have only two alternatives: obedience or disobedience. The decision confronting all of us alike is summed up, with characteristic logic, by the apostle Paul.

> God "will give to each person according to what he has done." To those who by persistence in doing good seek glory, honor and immortality, he will give eternal life. But for those who are self-seeking and who reject the truth and follow evil, there will be wrath and anger. There will be trouble and distress for every human being who does evil: first for the Jew, then for the Gentile; but glory, honor and peace for everyone who does good: first for the Jew, then for the Gentile. For God does not show favoritism.
>
> Romans 2:6–11

8

HOW SHALL WE RESPOND?

To this point, we have examined carefully a series of prophetic Scriptures that unfold God's predetermined purpose for the Jewish people and for the state of Israel. Out of these Scriptures, four main conclusions have emerged.

First, as this age draws to a close, God purposes to regather His scattered people Israel from all nations of the world and bring them back to their own land, there to make of them again one united nation.

Second, this geographical and political regathering is a prelude to the spiritual renewal of the Jewish people.

Third, this regathering and restoration began about the turn of the twentieth century and has been proceeding steadily ever since.

Fourth, the welfare of all nations is bound up with the fulfillment of God's plan to restore and renew Israel.

As Christians who accept the Bible's authority, we cannot ignore this clear revelation of God's purpose being worked out in our day. We are confronted, therefore, with a vitally important question: How shall we respond?

A Debt Compounded

Before we can attempt an adequate answer to this question, we must take into account two historical facts.

The first fact concerns all Christians of non-Jewish origin. Whatever our background may be—whether we are Africans or Arabs, Russians or Americans, Indians or Chinese—we all owe our entire spiritual inheritance as Christians to one nation—Israel.

If there had been no Israel, there would likewise have been no patriarchs, no prophets, no apostles, no Bible and no Savior. In John 4:22, Jesus Himself summed all this up in one simple statement: "Salvation is from the Jews." Christians from all other racial backgrounds owe to the Jewish people a spiritual debt that can never be calculated.

The second, related fact is that throughout most of its history, the Christian Church has not merely failed to repay its debt to Israel, it has actually compounded that debt many times over.

In chapter 2, I related how Christians in Britain recognized at various times God's purpose to restore the Jews to their land and sought to help and support them. Unfortunately, this kind of attitude on the part of Christians was exceptional.

In general, from about the fourth century on, the Christian Church has consistently treated the Jewish people with prejudice, contempt, injustice and even, at times, barbarous cruelty. Regrettably, the great majority of professing Christians today are almost totally ignorant of these historical facts, whereas they are indelibly engraved on the consciousness of the Jewish people and influence immeasurably their attitude toward Christianity.

As I have already indicated in chapter 2, one important cause of this Christian anti-Semitism was a warped form of theology, held widely in the Church for many centuries, that taught that the Jewish people were solely responsible for the crucifixion of Christ and were thus guilty of the most terrible of all crimes—the murder of God Himself.

On the basis of this theology, many Christians, including some recognized spiritual leaders, felt that one way to show their loyalty to Christ was to express their hatred toward His murderers—that is, the Jewish people.

For instance, even such a renowned preacher as John Chrysostom (c. AD 340–420), today regarded as a saint, could actually describe the Jewish people in his sermons as

> lustful, rapacious, greedy, perfidious bandits . . . inveterate murderers, destroyers, men possessed by the devil . . . Debauchery and drunkenness have given them the manners of the pig and the lusty goat. They know only one thing to satisfy their gullets, get drunk, to kill and maim one another.[8]

On another occasion Chrysostom said, "I hate the synagogue precisely because it has the law and the prophets. . . . I hate the Jews also because they outrage the law."[9]

The most tragic aspect of this is not that a renowned Christian theologian could espouse such sentiments toward the Jewish people—terrible though that is. Far more tragic is the fact that the utterances of Chrysostom, and others like him, had a profound effect upon the attitudes and the theology of many—perhaps even most—Christians for many centuries to come. This manifested itself in countless acts of violence and cruelty against the Jewish people. Christians who took part in the First Crusade at the end of the eleventh century, for example, turned aside on their way through Europe to the Middle East and massacred entire Jewish communities, sparing neither women nor children. After reaching Jerusalem, the Crusaders found an entire Jewish congregation gathered in a synagogue and proceeded to burn down the synagogue, killing all the Jews in it. All this was done in the name of Christ and in the sign of the cross.

Nor were the leaders of the Protestant Reformation free, by any means, from the guilt of anti-Jewish prejudice. When Martin Luther first published his teaching, he anticipated that the Jewish people would be convinced by it and would convert to Christianity. When this did not happen, Luther was disappointed and embittered. As a result, he actually outdid many Catholics in his vitriolic expressions of contempt for the Jewish people.

The scurrilous nature of some of Luther's attacks on the Jews is shocking. The following is a specimen of one of his more restrained utterances:

> The Jews deserve the most severe penalties. Their synagogues should be leveled, their homes destroyed, they should be exiled into tents like the gypsies. Their religious writings should be taken from them. The rabbis should be forbidden to continue teaching the Law. All professions should be closed to them. Only the hardest, coarsest work should be permitted them. Rich Jews should have their fortunes confiscated, and the money used to support Jews who are willing to be converted. If all these measures are unsuccessful, the Christian princes should have the duty of driving the Jews from their lands as they would rabid dogs.[10]

Centuries later, when the Nazis came to power in Germany, they used statements by Martin Luther to propagate anti-Semitic policies. The intensity of anti-Semitism that the Nazis succeeded in exploiting in Germany, and also in Poland, was not new; it had deep historical roots going back many centuries. And the main responsibility for this situation must be laid at the door of the Christian Church.

We could sum up the outworking of the historical processes involved by saying that the Nazis merely reaped a harvest that the Church had sown.

Accepting Our Responsibility

Confronted by this appalling record of anti-Semitism in the Christian Church throughout much of its history, modern Christians sometimes react by disclaiming any responsibility. "That was done by members of other churches," they protest. "In our church, we would never be guilty of such attitudes or acts."

I must confess that I, too, was inclined to shelter behind such an argument. But one day the Holy Spirit reminded me very forcefully of what Jesus said, in a similar context, to the religious leaders of His day:

> "Woe to you, teachers of the law and Pharisees, you hypocrites! You build tombs for the prophets and decorate the graves of the righteous. And you say, 'If we had lived in the days of our forefathers, we would not have taken part with them in shedding the blood of the prophets.' So you testify against yourselves that you are the descendants of those who murdered the prophets."
>
> Matthew 23:29–31

The very fact that these religious people disclaimed responsibility for the crimes committed by their forefathers against the prophets constituted an acknowledgment that they were indeed the descendants of those who had killed the prophets.

I believe the same principle applies to the crimes committed by the Church against the Jews. We cannot claim to be part of the Church and, at the same time, disclaim responsibility for the way the Church has treated the Jews. After all, in God's sight, there is only one Church.

If we desire to be identified with that one Church, then our identification must go all the way. We cannot claim inheritance in the good that has come down to us through the Church and yet, at the same time, disassociate ourselves from the evil. In particular, we must accept our share of responsibility for Christian anti-Semitism and then do everything in our power to rectify this terrible situation.

Pope John XXIII is one modern Christian leader who humbly acknowledged the guilt of the Church toward the Jews and sought to make amends. During World War II in Europe, as Archbishop Roncalli, he was instrumental in saving many Jews from the Nazis. Later, as Pope, he composed the following prayer of confession and repentance, intending it to be used in all Roman Catholic churches:

We are conscious today that many, many centuries of blindness have cloaked our eyes so that we can no longer see the beauty of Thy chosen people, nor recognize in their faces the features of our privileged brethren.

We realize that the mark of Cain stands upon our foreheads. Across the centuries our brother Abel has lain in the blood which we drew, or shed tears which we caused by forgetting Thy love.

Forgive us for the curse we falsely attached to their name as Jew.

Forgive us for crucifying Thee a second time in their flesh. For, O Lord, we know not what we did.[11]

I hope the Roman Catholic Church will still adopt this prayer for general use. My personal conviction is that the whole Christian Church, from every background and denomination, can never regain the full measure of divine blessing it has forfeited until it faces honestly the issue of its guilt toward the Jews and seeks to make amends.

One initial step is to correct the warped theology behind much Christian anti-Semitism. This theology overlooks two important facts that are stated clearly in the New Testament. First, the Jewish people were *not* solely responsible for the crucifixion of Jesus. They initiated the charges against Him, but it was the Romans who endorsed and carried out the sentence. It was Gentile Roman soldiers who were adding their own sadistic contribution to the total guilt of the human race. It is particularly strange that this fact so long escaped the attention of the *Roman* Catholic Church!

The second fact made clear in the New Testament is that, before He died on the cross, Jesus made provision for the forgiveness of all who had contributed to His suffering and death: "Father, forgive them, for they do not know what they are doing" (Luke 23:34). The word *them* includes all those responsible for Jesus's death, both Jew and Gentile.

In this light, all Christians today of non-Jewish background are confronted with two questions that cannot be evaded: First, what can we do to repay our spiritual debt to the Jewish people? And second, how can we—to some extent, at least—make amends for all the evil done to the Jewish people for centuries in the name of Christianity?

I believe the answer to these two questions is bound up in a special way with the outworking of God's purposes for Israel in our generation. We have before us an opportunity unique to our generation—one that is both an obligation and a privilege.

Our obligation is to do everything Scripture requires of us to help the Jewish people regain the fullness of their God-appointed inheritance, both natural and spiritual. Our privilege is to become co-workers with God in bringing about the fulfillment of His purposes of blessing for Israel and for all nations.

I want to suggest four specific ways, all of them indicated in Scripture, by which we can do this. They can be summed up by four verbs: to *praise*, to *proclaim*, to *pray* and to *comfort*.

To Praise

In Jeremiah 31, the prophet exhorts us to respond in three of these four ways to Israel's regathering: to praise, to proclaim and to pray. Someone has commented that this particular passage contains "one of the noisiest verses in the Bible." At the same time, to make the historical context absolutely clear, the prophet paints a vivid picture of the Jewish people being regathered to their land:

> This is what the LORD says:
>
> "Sing with joy for Jacob;
>   shout for the foremost of the nations.
> Make your praises heard, and say,
>   'O LORD, save your people,
>   the remnant of Israel.'
> See, I will bring them from the land of the north
>   and gather them from the ends of the earth.
> Among them will be the blind and the lame,
>   expectant mothers and women in labor;
>   a great throng will return."
>
> Jeremiah 31:7–8

One of the other modern versions offers a significant alternative for part of verse 7: "And shout *among the chiefs of the nations.* . . . *Proclaim*, give praise, and say" (NASB, emphasis added).

Both the words and the context of this prophecy leave no doubt that it refers to the end-time regathering and restoration of Israel. At the end of verse 7, we find the phrase *the remnant of Israel*—a phrase used regularly by the prophets in connection with this end-time regathering. Only a "remnant" of Israel will thus be regathered. In the aftermath of the Holocaust, the word remnant sounds a note of pathos.

The prophet then describes this regathering with a vividness and accuracy that could not be excelled even by a contemporary eyewitness of the events. We see once again the special emphasis on "the lands of the north," which include Germany, Poland and Russia.

But the remnant also comes from "the ends of the earth." This describes a phase in the history of Israel immediately following the War of Independence in 1948, which has come to be known by modern Israelis as the period of "mass immigration." Between 1948 and 1951, approximately 700,000 Jewish people immigrated to the state of Israel, mainly from Europe and the Arab nations, but also from many other lands (see special section, p. 146).

Of this total, about half were refugees from the Arab nations of the Middle East. In many cases, the refugees were expelled with ruthless haste and not permitted to take with them any money or material possessions, except for the clothes they were wearing. Most of these refugees had large families and came from an underprivileged level of society. The words of Jeremiah in verse 8 were exactly fulfilled hundreds of times over: "Among them . . . the blind and the lame, expectant mothers and women in labor; a great throng."

The period of history to which this refers is now. We cannot ignore the responses God requires of us. Let us look more closely, then, at the Scripture quoted above and its list of five responses:

1. To sing with joy
2. To shout
3. To proclaim
4. To praise (make our praises heard)
5. To say (or pray), "O Lord, save your people."

We may combine under the single heading of "praise" three of the responses listed above: to sing with joy, to shout and to praise. Taken together, these three phrases describe loud, sustained, exuberant praise.

Why should we respond with this kind of praise to Israel's regathering? Let me suggest three practical reasons.

First, quite simply, because almighty God Himself requires it of us. That in itself is sufficient reason. To respond as God requires is obedience; to fail to respond is disobedience. Obedience will bring God's blessing upon us, and disobedience will bring His judgment. In order to receive God's blessing and avoid His judgment, we are obligated to respond as He requires.

Second, we should respond with praise because, as we have already seen, the contemporary regathering of Israel is objective confirmation on a worldwide scale that the Bible is true, relevant and up-to-date.

As Christians, we, just like Israel, depend upon the mercy and faithfulness of God promised to us in the Bible. There is probably nothing in all of the Scriptures to which God commits Himself more repeatedly than this end-time regathering of His chosen people. If God does not fulfill His repeated commitments to Israel, then I, for my part, could no longer have confidence that He will fulfill His commitments to the Church.

The fact that God is manifestly fulfilling His commitments to Israel should be the greatest possible encouragement that He will also fulfill His commitments to us as Christians. Therefore, praise is our natural and logical response.

Third, praise is also the natural, appropriate expression of Christian compassion. When we remember the long centuries of Israel's anguish, most of it inflicted by Christians and culminating in the unthinkable horrors of the Holocaust, we would betray the stoniness of our own hearts if we did not continually praise God that their night of anguish is drawing to a close and that a new day of restoration and peace is dawning.

God is specific about the kind of praise He requires of us. It is not to be something merely inward and inaudible. On the contrary, God says that we are to sing, to shout, to make our praises heard.

Today, perhaps more than ever before, the world is filled with all sorts of negative voices—voices of discontent, strife, hatred, blasphemy; voices that rob God of the glory due His name. As Christians, we have the obligation and the privilege to drown out these negative voices with our sustained and jubilant praises, thus restoring to God the glory that is His due. As we do this, we create a spiritual atmosphere in which it becomes easier for both Israel and the Church to enter into their God-appointed inheritance.

To Proclaim

The word *proclaim* means to make some kind of public, official declaration. It suggests, in particular, the activity of a herald. The kind of proclamation we are to make is defined further on in Jeremiah 31:

> "Hear the word of the LORD, O nations;
>   proclaim it in distant coastlands:
> 'He who scattered Israel will gather them
>   and will watch over his flock like a shepherd.'"

> verse 10

Our message need not be lengthy or complicated. Its essence is this: "He who scattered Israel will gather them." (In the original Hebrew, it is briefer still. In fact, it consists of three words: first word, *He-who-scattered*; second word, *Israel*; third word, *will-gather-them*—literally, *him*.) God wastes no words! He does not permit any secondary issue to divert us from that which is central: His regathering of scattered Israel.

Jeremiah's words leave no room for misunderstanding. The same God who scattered Israel will be the One to gather them. There can be no change in the identity of God (as we saw in chapter 5). The same people who were scattered, Israel, will be the ones to be gathered. There can be no change in the identity of Israel. The scattering took place literally in a series of events in human history; likewise, the gathering will take place literally in the events of human history, exactly as described in Scripture.

Let me point out another interesting fact that confirms in an amazing way the absolute accuracy of biblical prophecy. The Hebrew word used here for "gathering" comes from a basic verb form: *kibbetz*. The same basic form also gives us the modern Hebrew word *kibbutz* (of which the plural is *kibbutzim*).

A kibbutz may be defined roughly as a group of people who settle together on an area of land, pool their resources and lead a communal kind of life. The original emphasis of nearly all *kibbutzim* in Israel was primarily agricultural, although today there have been other developments. It is an objective fact of history that the *kibbutzim* have played a unique and vital part in the growth of modern Israel. They have made an indispensable contribution to both the economy and the defense of the state.

With these linguistic and historical facts in mind, we may paraphrase Jeremiah 31:10 as follows: "He who scattered Israel will regather them in *kibbutzim*." Is it not remarkable that, twenty-five centuries before their occurrence, the prophet Jeremiah predicted these events accurately and even used in his prediction a word that singled out one of their most significant features?

In the closing section of the proclamation, Jeremiah says that the Lord will also "watch over his flock like a shepherd." The word translated "watch over" also means "keep" or "guard." Here is further confirmation that this second regathering of Israel will not be something temporary or transient. Once God has gathered them, He will continue to watch over and protect them. As their Shepherd, He will accept responsibility for their permanent security and well-being.

To whom is this proclamation addressed? It is addressed to "nations" and to "distant coastlands." The Hebrew word translated *nations* usually denotes nations other than Israel and is used regularly by Jewish people to describe the Gentiles. The word translated *coastlands* would include *islands* and *continents*. Today, through the Holy Spirit, God is raising up a company of ministers of His Word to whom He is committing the task of carrying this proclamation to all the places here indicated by Jeremiah.

In recent years it has been my privilege to make this proclamation in the United States and in various countries around the world—some within the continent of Europe and others that were formerly part of the British Empire. Among the former are Germany, Switzerland and Sweden. Among the latter are England, Northern Ireland, Australia, New Zealand, Jamaica and South Africa. In each of these places, I have directed people's attention to this specific verse in Jeremiah 31:10, and then I have said to them, "Today this Scripture is being fulfilled in your ears."

Today, the regathering of Israel is a banner lifted up by God for all nations to see. It is His preordained purpose at this time that all nations be confronted with this message. And there is an important reason: When God's time comes to judge the nations, He will judge them on the basis of their response to the regathering of Israel. At that time, no nation will be able to plead ignorance of Israel's regathering or of the fact that it represents the fulfillment of God's prophetic Word.

To Pray

Prayer, our third response, is indicated by the words at the end of Jeremiah 31:7: "Say, 'O LORD, save your people, the remnant of Israel.'"

We must realize that when God grants us a revelation of what He is intending to do in the world, His purpose is never merely to interest or entertain us. He does not expect us to remain passive or indifferent. On the contrary, He requires us to become actively, wholeheartedly involved in carrying out His revealed intention, by whatever means are appropriate to our particular situation. A primary way is through prayer. An excellent example of this kind of commitment is found in the book of Daniel:

> In the first year of Darius son of Xerxes (a Mede by descent), who was made ruler over the Babylonian kingdom—in the first year of his reign, I, Daniel, understood from the Scriptures, according to the word of the LORD given to Jeremiah the prophet, that the desolation of Jerusalem would last seventy years. So I turned to the Lord God and pleaded with him in prayer and petition, in fasting, and in sackcloth and ashes.
>
> Daniel 9:1–3

We see here that Daniel was not merely a prophet; he was also a student of prophecy. (If the facts were available to us, I believe this would also prove true of the other great prophets of the Bible.) The Scriptures to which Daniel refers are Jeremiah 25:12–14 and 29:10–14. Through his study of these two passages, Daniel understood that the Lord was about to put an end to the Jews' captivity in Babylon and open the way for them to return to their own land.

Daniel thus found himself in a position parallel to that in which we find ourselves today. How did he respond?

Certainly he was not passive or indifferent. On the contrary, he gave himself to prayer and fasting more earnest and intense than anything previously recorded in the book of Daniel. His prayer was that God would indeed fulfill the promises of mercy He had given through the prophet Jeremiah to Israel.

In this, Daniel stands as a pattern and challenge to us today. This second worldwide regathering of Israel, far greater than the first, calls for prayer and fasting on a corresponding worldwide scale.

In Isaiah 62, God calls us to intense, persistent prayer, especially on behalf of Jerusalem:

> I have posted watchmen on your walls, O Jerusalem;
>   they will never be silent day or night.
> You who call on the LORD,
>   give yourselves no rest,
> and give him no rest till he establishes Jerusalem
>   and makes her the praise of the earth.
>
> Isaiah 62:6–7

Clearly, these "watchmen" are intercessors, called by God to continue in prayer day and night for the restoration of Jerusalem.

In the New Testament, Jesus relates the parable of the widow who kept beseeching the unjust judge. Then He concludes with this question: "And will not God bring about justice for his chosen ones, who cry out to him day and night?" (Luke 18:7).

Both these passages indicate that some themes are so important and urgent that they demand our prayers not only in the daytime, but through the night hours as well. The restoration of Jerusalem is one of these themes. The metaphor of "watchmen" suggests people whose commitment to their task requires them to remain alert and at their post throughout the hours of darkness.

Isaiah also describes these "watchmen" as those "who call on the Lord." The Hebrew word thus translated is interesting. It means, literally, "those who remind the Lord." In modern Hebrew, it is the word for a secretary.

One day I was wondering about the connection between this ministry of calling on the Lord and the task of a secretary. Then I realized that one important part of a secretary's task is to remind the employer of the appointments recorded on his calendar.

This gave me practical insight into the way God wants us to pray for Jerusalem. As His "intercessor-secretaries," we have two main responsibilities: first, to be familiar with His prophetic calendar; and second, to remind Him of the appointments recorded in it. One such appointment is God's end-time commitment to restore Israel and to rebuild Jerusalem.

The exhortation to pray for the peace of this city is not confined to the critical period at the close of the present age. It appears continuously through Scripture and through the history of God's people, from the time of David onward. In Psalm 122, David says:

> Pray for the peace of Jerusalem:
> "May they prosper who love you.
> May peace be within your walls,
> And prosperity within your palaces."
>
> verses 6–7, NASB

Every day through nineteen centuries, the Jewish people in all the lands of their exile have obeyed faithfully this exhortation to pray for the peace of Jerusalem. The dramatic events that have taken place in Jerusalem from 1948 onward are history's testimony that God has not forgotten these many centuries of prayer.

We might be tempted to ask, Why should God's believing people around the world be exhorted by Scripture to pray for this one city, Jerusalem?

One reason at least is clear: Scripture reveals that it is God's ultimate purpose to establish His Kingdom on earth with Jerusalem as
its center. It is this we are praying for each time we utter the familiar
words, "Thy kingdom come."

It is outside the scope of this book to develop the theme of
God's Kingdom in detail. But let us take a few quick glimpses at
what God has in store for all who qualify for admission to that
Kingdom.

Here is just one passage from Isaiah:

This is what Isaiah son of Amoz saw concerning Judah and
Jerusalem:

In the last days

> the mountain of the LORD's temple will be established
>> as chief among the mountains;
> it will be raised above the hills,
>> and all nations will stream to it.

Many peoples will come and say,

> "Come, let us go up to the mountain of the LORD,
>> to the house of the God of Jacob.
> He will teach us his ways,
>> so that we may walk in his paths."
> The law will go out from Zion,
>> the word of the LORD from Jerusalem.
> He will judge between the nations
>> and will settle disputes for many peoples.
> They will beat their swords into plowshares
>> and their spears into pruning hooks.
> Nation will not take up sword against nation,
>> nor will they train for war anymore.

Isaiah 2:1–4

And this is from the prophet Zechariah:

On that day living water will flow out from Jerusalem, half to the eastern sea and half to the western sea, in summer and in winter.

The LORD will be king over the whole earth. On that day there will be one LORD, and his name the only name. . . .

Then the survivors from all the nations that have attacked Jerusalem will go up year after year to worship the King, the LORD Almighty, and to celebrate the Feast of Tabernacles.

Zechariah 14:8–9, 16

These prophetic pictures of God's Kingdom established on earth have one feature in common: Jerusalem, or Mount Zion, is at the center. It is to Jerusalem that all nations will go up each year for worship. It is from Jerusalem that the Word and Law of the Lord will go forth and that justice and government will be administered to all nations.

In this way, the peace and well-being of all nations are inseparably bound up with the peace of Jerusalem. Until Jerusalem enters into her own peace, no other city or land anywhere on earth can be secure from the threat of war, nor can the nations know true and lasting happiness.

Thus, in praying for the peace of Jerusalem, Christians from nations all over the globe are also praying for a consummation that will bring peace and incalculable blessings to their own nations.

There is yet another reason we should all be eager to pray for the peace of Jerusalem. God has ordained that those who love Jerusalem and who, in obedience to His Word, pray for her peace shall "prosper." The word here translated "to prosper" goes beyond material prosperity. It is alternatively translated to "be secure," and it includes inner rest and well-being.

Over many years now, I have made a practice of praying regularly for the peace of Jerusalem. Out of personal experience, I can testify that God has been faithful to grant me the full reward He promised.

To Comfort

Our fourth response to Israel's regathering is to comfort the Jewish people, especially at this most critical juncture in their history. This is unfolded in Isaiah 40:1–8, a passage that falls naturally into three successive sections, distinct but logically interconnected.

The first section, consisting of verses 1–2, opens with our key word, *comfort*:

> Comfort, comfort my people,
>   says your God.
> Speak tenderly to Jerusalem,
>   and proclaim to her
> that her hard service has been completed,
>   that her sin has been paid for,
> that she has received from the LORD's hand
>   double for all her sins.

The opening verbs of both verses—*comfort* and *speak*—are in the plural, addressed not to an individual but to a group of people. Thus, we have in these verses two distinct groups. God calls one group "My people" and, as we have already seen, He is referring to the Jews. The other group consists of those who are charged to be the comforters of "My people."

The message of comfort to "My people" is also a message of comfort to Jerusalem, which is consistent with the historical attitude of the Jewish people. Throughout the nineteen centuries of their exile, they have never ceased to grieve over Jerusalem's desolation or to pray for her restoration.

The eternal, unchanging dedication of the Jewish people to Jerusalem's welfare is summed up in the words of Psalm 137:

> If I forget you, O Jerusalem,
> May my right hand forget her skill.
> May my tongue cleave to the roof of my mouth,
> If I do not remember you,
> If I do not exalt Jerusalem
> Above my chief joy.
>
> verses 5–6, NASB

Any message that promises comfort to the Jewish people must, at the same time, promise comfort to Jerusalem. Otherwise, the comfort would be hollow and incomplete.

There is no segment of humanity whose need of comfort can even be compared with that of the Jewish people. Through the course of history, many other racial and religious groups have been the victims of prejudice and persecution. But the sufferings of the Jewish people far exceed all others in their scope, intensity and duration. In the wisdom and mercy of God, He promises them not only regathering, but also comfort.

In another picture of Israel's restoration, the psalmist brings together both these aspects of God's mercy:

> The LORD builds up Jerusalem;
>   he gathers the exiles of Israel.
> He heals the brokenhearted
>   and binds up their wounds.
>
> Psalm 147:2–3

The rebuilding of Jerusalem and the regathering of Israel's exiles will thus be consummated by the healing of the brokenhearted and the binding up of their wounds.

But if "My people" denotes Israel, then who is the other group of people, those exhorted in Isaiah 40:1 to comfort Israel? Clearly they are not Israel; yet they believe in the God who speaks to them through the prophets of Israel, and they accept His prophetic Word as authoritative in their lives. I know of only one group of people who answer to this description. It is the whole body of Christians worldwide who accept the Bible as God's Word and are committed to obeying it. It is to them that God now says, "Comfort my people. . . . Speak tenderly to Jerusalem."

By their faith in Scripture and by the revelation of the Holy Spirit, Christians can already affirm with confidence that which is not yet fully manifested in the events of history: The sufferings of Israel and the desolations of Jerusalem are coming to an end. A new day of mercy is dawning.

In the second section of his prophecy—chapter 40:3–5—Isaiah issues a call to prepare the way for the Lord:

> A voice of one calling:
> "In the desert prepare
>   the way for the LORD;
> make straight in the wilderness
>   a highway for our God.
> Every valley shall be raised up,
>   every mountain and hill made low;
> the rough ground shall become level,
>   the rugged places a plain.
> And the glory of the LORD will be revealed,
>   and all mankind together will see it.
>   For the mouth of the LORD has spoken."

Verse 3 tells us that this message of comfort to Israel serves to "prepare the way for the LORD." For each of the two comings of the Messiah, a special ministry is needed to prepare the hearts of His people so that they may be ready to receive Him. The New Testament reveals that it was the ministry of John the Baptist that prepared the way for the first coming of Jesus (see Mark 1:1–4).

Before the second coming of Jesus, there will once again be a special ministry needed to prepare the hearts of Israel. This ministry, like that of John, will call for repentance, but it will also promise comfort to those who repent. God is calling Bible-believing Christians worldwide to take part in this end-time ministry of preparing the hearts of Israel for their Messiah.

Verse 4 warns of tremendous changes associated with the return of Jesus. Valleys will be raised up; mountains will be brought down; rough, rugged ground will be leveled. These cataclysmic upheavals represent the climax of the "birth pains" that will usher in a new age.

Similar topographical descriptions are found in related Scriptures such as Isaiah 2:2 and Zechariah 14:4 and 10. Certainly these passages describe actual changes that will take place. But they also carry a wider significance.

Much that is arrogant and highly esteemed in our contemporary culture will be cast down by God's judgments on human pride. Some nations that appear to dominate today's world will be humiliated and may even pass from the scene altogether. Other nations that are considered weak or insignificant today will be elevated to positions of honor and prosperity. This will fulfill the statement of Jesus in Matthew 5:5: "Blessed are the meek, for they will inherit the earth."

Verse 5 of Isaiah 40 unfolds the consummation to which all God's end-time purposes are directed: the revelation of His glory to the entire human race. A similar picture is found later on in Isaiah:

> From the west, men will fear the name of the LORD,
>   and from the rising of the sun, they will revere his glory. . . .
>
> "The Redeemer will come to Zion,
>   to those in Jacob who repent of their sins,"
>   declares the LORD.
>
> Isaiah 59:19–20

Each of these two passages from Isaiah ends with an emphatic declaration that it is God Himself who promises to reveal His glory to the whole earth. In Isaiah 40:5, the closing phrase is, "For the mouth of the LORD has spoken." In Isaiah 59:20, the closing phrase is "declares the LORD." With this special form of emphasis, God Himself accepts the responsibility for the fulfillment of what is predicted.

Isaiah climaxes the third section of this prophetic passage—chapter 40:6–8—with the actual message of comfort that is to be delivered to Israel:

> A voice says, "Cry out."
>   And I said, "What shall I cry?"
>
> "All men are like grass,
>   and all their glory is like the flowers of the field.
> The grass withers and the flowers fall,
>   because the breath of the LORD blows on them.

> Surely the people are grass.
> The grass withers and the flowers fall,
> but the word of our God stands forever."

The prophet inquires here what his message of comfort shall be, and he is told, "All men are like grass."

At first we may wonder what kind of comfort this is. It speaks of the frailty and impermanence of all human strength and glory. All is doomed to wither and pass away, just like the grass and the flowers.

Furthermore, the grass and the flowers wither "because the breath of the LORD blows on them." God Himself puts an end to their life. Likewise, He puts an end to all human strength and glory. All our experience confirms that this is true, although we are often reluctant to face up to it.

But what comfort is there in such a message?

The comfort is found in the closing phrase: "But the word of our God stands forever." First, God confronts us with the frailty and impermanence of all human existence. Then He leads us on to the one element in human experience that is permanent and unchanging: His own Word, the Scriptures. Herein lies the only message of hope and comfort for the Jewish people.

For more than two thousand years, they have seen a long procession of kingdoms and civilizations pass across the stage of human history. Most have been, in some measure, unkind or hostile to the Jewish people. Some have actually sought their total destruction. But, just like the grass and the flowers, all their strength and glory have withered and fallen, leaving behind only the records and relics of history. When all these have passed, two things remain upon the stage of history: God's eternal, unchanging Word and the Jewish people, whose survival is guaranteed by that Word.

I am reminded of a cartoon I saw in a newspaper shortly after World War II. The scene was a graveyard. A long line of tombstones stretched away toward the far end. On the newest tombstone, nearest to the front, was engraved a swastika and the name of Adolf Hitler. In the forefront was a freshly dug grave in which no one had yet been buried, and beside it stood an elderly orthodox Jew.

In the caption underneath the cartoon were his words: "Who will be the next?"

Here, then, is our message of comfort to Israel at this time of their regathering and restoration. All the rulers and nations who have oppressed and persecuted them will come to naught. Their glory will wither, just like that of the flowers and the grass.

But the Word of Israel's God, spoken to them through their own prophets, stands eternal and unchanging. This Word, that promises judgment to Israel's oppressors, also promises mercy to Israel. Just as the promises of judgment have been fulfilled, so surely will the promises of mercy also be fulfilled.

To Christians ready to obey God and bring this message of comfort to Israel, Isaiah 40:9 offers strong encouragement:

> You who bring good tidings to Zion,
>   go up on a high mountain.
> You who bring good tidings to Jerusalem,
>   lift up your voice with a shout,
> lift it up, do not be afraid;
>   say to the towns of Judah,
>   "Here is your God!"

9

THE JUDGMENT
OF NATIONS

From the many passages of Scripture we have examined in chapters 4 through 8, God's plan for the close of this age has emerged with great clarity. Through His prophetic Word, God has declared to all nations that He intends to regather Israel in their own land and restore them to His favor. He has also made it clear that He will intervene in judgment against those nations who oppress Israel or resist God's purposes for them.

The issues that thus confront all nations are set forth clearly in Joel:

> "In those days and at that time,
>   when I restore the fortunes of Judah and Jerusalem,
> I will gather all nations
>   and bring them down to the Valley of Jehoshaphat."
>
> Joel 3:1–2

Here, like two sides of a coin, the prophet sets forth the two opposite aspects of God's dealings with the nations at the close of this age: mercy and restoration for Israel, but judgment for all those nations who oppose and oppress Israel and claim jurisdiction over Israel's land.

The place ordained for judgment is called "the Valley of Jehoshaphat." This is an actual location, but the name also carries symbolic meaning, since *Jehoshaphat* means "the Lord judges."

In this same chapter of Joel, God makes two further references to this valley of judgment:

> "Let the nations be roused;
>   let them advance into the Valley of Jehoshaphat,
> for there I will sit
>   to judge all the nations on every side."

verse 12

> Multitudes, multitudes
>   in the valley of decision!
> For the day of the LORD is near
>   in the valley of decision.

verse 14

The Valley of Decision

We see, then, that "the valley of the Lord's judgment" is also "the valley of decision." What are we to understand by this latter phrase? For me, it depicts a valley that God, through the pressure of world events, will compel all nations to enter. Once they have entered it, they will not be able to leave until they have made a decision. A decision will be the only way out.

The decision required of all nations will be simple. They must either submit to God's Word or reject it. Submission will entail aligning themselves with God's revealed purposes for Israel. Opposing God's purposes for Israel will constitute rejection of His Word and will inevitably bring the judgment He forewarns.

Many other prophetic passages of Scripture likewise indicate that, at the close of this age, God will judge the nations on the basis of their attitude toward the regathering of Israel and the accompanying restoration of their land and of the city of Jerusalem.

There is a whole series of related verses in Isaiah 60:

> "Lift up your eyes and look about you:
>   All assemble and come to you;
> your sons come from afar,
>   and your daughters are carried on the arm."
>
> verse 4

> "Foreigners will rebuild your walls,
>   and their kings will serve you."
>
> verse 10

> "For the nation or kingdom that will not serve you will perish;
>   it will be utterly ruined."
>
> verse 12

> "The sons of your oppressors will come bowing before you;
>   all who despise you will bow down at your feet
> and will call you the City of the LORD,
>   Zion of the Holy One of Israel.
>
> "Although you have been forsaken and hated,
>   with no one traveling through,
> I will make you the everlasting pride
>   and the joy of all generations."
>
> verses 14–15

First, we need to establish the historical context of this prophecy. Verse 4 uses language similar to many other pictures of the regathering of scattered Israel in their own land. Then, in verse 14, the prophet uses the specific title *Zion*. In the same verse, the phrase *the sons of your oppressors* describes the descendants of those nations that have persecuted Israel.

Again in verse 15, the statement *you have been forsaken and hated, with no one traveling through* clearly describes Israel and the city of Jerusalem during the period of their desolation.

All the above verses leave no doubt that this prophetic passage is addressed to Zion—a title referring primarily to the city of Jerusalem and, by extension, to the land and people of Israel.

With this in mind, we can now examine the verses at the heart of the passage quoted above—verses 10 and 12. Each shows the attitude and response that God requires from all rulers and nations to the restoration of Israel and of Jerusalem. Verse 10 presents this from a positive aspect: "Foreigners will rebuild your walls, and their kings will serve you." Verse 12 presents this same truth from a negative aspect: "For the nation or kingdom that will not serve you will perish; it will be utterly ruined."

Thus Israel is the "watershed," the line of separation between nations. Rulers and nations will determine their own destiny by how they respond to what God does for Israel.

In a measure, this has already proven true many times in history. In the fifteenth and sixteenth centuries, for example, Spain was the dominant nation of Europe, with a high level of culture, a powerful army and navy and an empire that spanned both hemispheres. Within a century of expelling all Jews from her territories, Spain declined to a struggling, second-rate power.

In my personal memory and experience, much the same happened to my own motherland, Britain. Britain emerged victorious from two world wars, retaining intact an empire that was perhaps the most extensive in human history. But in 1947–48, as the mandatory power over Palestine, Britain opposed and attempted to thwart the rebirth of Israel as a sovereign nation.

From that very moment in history, Britain's empire underwent a process of decline and disintegration so rapid and total that it cannot be accounted for by merely the relevant political, military or economic factors. Today, less than a generation later, Britain—like Spain—has lost her world supremacy.

On a more recent note, one of the largest and cruelest empires of the twentieth century, the Soviet Union, took an active stand against Israel and prevented Soviet Jews from immigrating to Israel.

Countless believers around the world interceded for the ingathering of the Jews from the "land of the north" (Jeremiah 16:14–15; see also Isaiah 43:5–6). The Lord intervened and brought the total disintegration of this once-mighty empire and the release of almost a million Soviet Jews.

God's dealings with the nations over the issue of Israel illustrate a basic principle that underlies His dealings with mankind as a whole. When God deals with man, He does not step down from His throne and confront each individual in His own Person. Rather, He confronts man indirectly through His Word. In this way, our response to God's Word becomes our response to God Himself—even though we ourselves may not recognize it.

This has been true from the very outset of human history. When God placed Adam in the garden, He did not remain there continuously present in person, supervising his conduct. Rather, from that point onward, God was represented by the word that He left with Adam: "You are free to eat from any tree in the garden; but you must not eat from the tree of the knowledge of good and evil, for when you eat of it you will surely die" (Genesis 2:16–17).

When Adam disobeyed this word from God, the consequences were just the same as if He had disobeyed God to His face. Rejecting God's word was equivalent to rejecting God in person.

The same principle recurs many times in God's dealings with Israel. At one point, for example, God spoke to King Saul through the prophet Samuel, charging him to execute His judgment on the Amalekites. When Saul failed to carry out the whole charge, Samuel told him, "Because you have rejected the word of the LORD, he has rejected you as king" (1 Samuel 15:23).

For Saul to reject God's Word through His prophet Samuel was precisely the same as if he had rejected God Himself. It cost Saul his throne and, ultimately, his life.

When God thus confronts a man or nation through His Word, He Himself chooses the issue on which He focuses. With Adam, it was the fruit of a tree. With Saul, it was executing judgment on the Amalekites. Whatever the issue, behind it lies God's ultimate requirement of submission and obedience to His Word.

So it is with the judgment of the nations. God Himself has chosen the issue: the restoration of Israel. It would seem that, in focusing on Israel, God has deliberately chosen a people who are apparently weak and who have been persistently rejected by other nations. In this way, the decision each nation makes concerning Israel is not likely to be clouded by possible considerations of expedience or material self-interest.

Thus there remains only one unchanging and sufficient reason for nations to align themselves with Israel: God has revealed clearly in His Word that He intends to restore Israel and that He requires all other nations to cooperate with His purpose. Any nation that rejects this revelation of God's Word has, in effect, rejected God Himself and must suffer the consequences.

The Sheep and the Goats

The principle of judging the nations that is unfolded here is not confined to the Old Testament. In the New Testament, Jesus Himself reveals that when He returns in glory as King to set up His Kingdom, He will judge the nations by the same principle.

In Matthew 25, He depicts vividly the judgment that will take place at that time. In this parable—which is, more accurately, a prophecy—Jesus employs the simile of a shepherd separating his sheep from his goats. The question to be settled at this judgment is: Which nations will be counted worthy to take their place in the Kingdom that Jesus is setting up, and which nations will be excluded from it?

Jesus sets the "sheep" nations on His right hand and welcomes them into His Kingdom with the words, "Come, ye blessed of my Father, inherit the kingdom prepared for you" (verse 34, KJV). On His left, He sets the "goat" nations, excluding them from the Kingdom with the words, "Depart from me, ye cursed, into everlasting fire" (verse 41). The principle by which the "sheep" are separated from the "goats" is simple: *It is the way they have treated the brothers of Jesus.* The "sheep" nations have shown them mercy wherever they have encountered them in situations of need—whether hungry, thirsty, strangers, naked, sick or imprisoned. In similar situations, conversely, the "goat" nations have failed to show them mercy.

In each case, Jesus declares that the way these nations have treated His brothers is reckoned as the way they have treated Jesus Himself. Mercy shown to them is mercy shown to Him, and mercy withheld from them is mercy withheld from Him. It follows, therefore, that nations determine their own destiny by the way they treat the brothers of Jesus.

The New Testament reveals that the brothers of Jesus fall into two categories: those related to Him through flesh and blood and those related to Him as committed disciples. At a certain point in His ministry, He looked at the disciples seated around Him and said, "Here are my mother and my brothers! Whoever does God's will is my brother and sister and mother" (Mark 3:34). Thus, Jesus includes all true disciples as members of His family.

He was not excluding, however, those related to Him by flesh and blood. As I pointed out in chapter 1, Jesus continues throughout eternity to be "the Lion of the tribe of Judah, the Root of David" (Revelation 5:5). He is forever identified with the family of David and the tribe of Judah, and He still retains the special identification this gives Him with the Jewish people.

Thus, the brothers of Jesus referred to in the picture of the sheep and goats may be taken to include both Christians and Jews. Understood in this way, the principle of separation between sheep and goats applies directly to the period in which we now live. All the elements of the situation Jesus depicted are already present in contemporary world politics.

Two aspects of that situation are particularly significant. First, the single most controversial and divisive issue in world politics today is the state of Israel. Opposition to Israel is headed by a bloc of Muslim nations that have not only refused to recognize Israel's existence, but are actually committed to its destruction. These nations carry more influence than they normally would because they control a major share of the world's supply of oil, upon which all modern nations are dependent.

While the extreme control of the communists in the former Soviet Union has been broken, virulent anti-Semitism is still widespread in that region. These enemies of Israel are so aggressive in the pressures they exert that it is increasingly difficult for other nations to follow policies favorable to Israel or even maintain an attitude of neutrality.

More and more, those nations that continue to support Israel will do so not on the basis of material self-interest but on that of moral and religious conviction. This will be one important aspect of conduct required to qualify them, as nations, for a place in Christ's Kingdom on earth.

A second critical element in contemporary world politics is that the ideologies of Islam and communism, which head the opposition to Israel, are also the two most powerful spiritual forces that oppose Christianity in today's world. As an ideology, each is committed by its basic doctrine to achieve ultimate world domination. If either were to succeed in this—and it would not matter which group it was—it would spell the end of Christianity.

A third force on the rise that is already opposing Israel is secular humanism. This force is more subtle because it speaks of unity and peace but opposes God's sovereignty and purposes as stated in the prophetic Scriptures for Israel. This power increasingly influences the Western nations, as well as Israel itself, and has set the stage for increased pressure on Israel to give up the land promised Israel by God in His covenant to Abraham in exchange for "peace" with its Arab neighbors.

Most Christians are aware, to some degree, of the anti-Christian nature of atheistic communism. Many have little or no idea, however, of the true attitude of Islam toward Christianity. In the last resort, the spirit and goals of Islam are opposed more intractably to Christianity than even those of atheistic communism.

In nations once controlled by communism, it is still possible today to find some Christian churches that are actually flourishing. But in nations dominated by Islam, a flourishing Christian church can scarcely be found.

In the midst of these anti-Christian pressures, however, the prophetic Word of God continues to shape the course of history. Even as Islamic and communist ideologies strive against God's Word, they are, without knowing it, instruments to bring it to fulfillment.

Like a vast pair of pincers, they are at work throughout the world, forcing Christians and Jews together. In this way, they are helping to put an end to the centuries-old separation between "the brothers of Jesus"—those born according to the Spirit and those born according to the flesh.

Confronted by these powerful common enemies, Christians and Jews are being compelled to reevaluate their attitudes toward one another. Rather than focusing on the points that have kept them apart for so long, they are beginning to emphasize the many elements of their common spiritual heritage.

The powerful spiritual renewal affecting the Christian Church worldwide has caused Christians from all backgrounds to return to their basic biblical origins. They have thus discovered, often to their surprise, that in Old and New Testament alike, these origins are Jewish.

The state of Israel, on the other hand, confronted with the defection of many of its former political allies, is beginning to realize—with at least equal surprise—that its firmest and most influential friends today are found among Bible-believing Christians worldwide.

In this way, the lines are being drawn for the final conflict destined to usher in God's Kingdom on earth. The divinely appointed representatives of that Kingdom, both Christian and Jewish, find themselves standing side by side. All the forces that oppose God's Kingdom are lining up against them.

The conflict spans two realms—the natural and the spiritual. Christians are called to play their part primarily in the spiritual realm. (Recall, in chapter 8, the four spiritual responsibilities of Christians: praise, proclamation, prayer and comfort.) In the natural realm, the conflict focuses mainly on the land and the people of Israel.

The Stage Is Set

On the stage of human history, the final phases of the conflict are described in the three closing chapters of Zechariah. In the first of these three chapters, Zechariah 12, the Lord introduces Himself in all His omnipotence and omniscience:

> This is the word of the LORD concerning Israel. The LORD, who stretches out the heavens, who lays the foundation of the earth, and who forms the spirit of man within him, declares.
>
> verse 1

Here the Lord gives two reasons why He can both control and predict the course of history. First, He is the Creator of heaven and earth, who continues to control all He has created. Second, He forms the spirit of man within him; He knows the thoughts and intentions of all men. No individual or nation can form any plan that is hidden from the Lord.

The New Testament likewise declares God's omniscience, presenting it as a function of His Word:

> The word of God is living and active. Sharper than any double-edged sword, it penetrates even to dividing soul and spirit, joints and marrow; it judges the thoughts and attitudes of the heart. Nothing in all creation is hidden from God's sight. Everything is uncovered and laid bare before the eyes of him to whom we must give account.
>
> Hebrews 4:12–13

The writer pictures God's Word as a kind of spiritual X-ray, discerning all that is inside man. It is reasonable, then, that the same Word of God that uncovers man's innermost thoughts can also predict how he will behave in any given situation.

Returning now to Zechariah 12, we see God setting the stage for the final conflict:

> "I am going to make Jerusalem a cup that sends all the surrounding peoples reeling. Judah will be besieged as well as Jerusalem."
>
> verse 2

The central issue around which the conflict ultimately revolves, according to the prophet, is the city of Jerusalem—which corresponds with the present situation in world politics. In 1947, when the United Nations voted to partition Palestine, they proposed that Jerusalem be declared an international city. In the ensuing fighting, however, the Jews retained control over the western section of the city, while Jordan annexed the eastern section, including the Old City and the Temple area.

Then, in the Six-Day War in 1967, Israel gained control of the entire city and, subsequently, declared Jerusalem to be "the eternal capital" of the state of Israel. Anyone familiar with the innermost convictions of the Jewish people can vouch for one certainty: *Israel will never voluntarily yield up control of Jerusalem.*

Zechariah goes on to describe the reaction of "all the surrounding peoples." These are, of course, all the Muslim nations of the Middle East. For them, Jerusalem under Jewish control has become "a cup that sends them reeling."

The Jerusalem Bible renders this phrase "an intoxicating cup"—a drink that is so intoxicating that the nations who taste it no longer retain full control of their actions. They can no longer act rationally but are like people who are either drunk or drugged.

This intoxicating ingredient is already at work among the Muslim peoples. It could perhaps be defined as "demonic fanaticism." It has called forth attitudes and utterances so extreme and hateful that they cannot be considered fully rational.

This ingredient has provoked a call by various Muslim leaders and nations for a united jihad—holy war—to recover Jerusalem from the Jewish people. So far, however, the endless rivalries of the Muslim peoples have kept them from uniting effectively to carry out their purpose.

In Zechariah's picture, the conflict concerning Jerusalem is set in the context of a siege: "Judah will be besieged as well as Jerusalem."

When I was in Jerusalem in 1947–48, I witnessed what I felt to be an initial fulfillment of this prediction. Both the Jewish section of Jerusalem and the Jewish community (that is to say, Judah) were, for a time, besieged by the surrounding Arabs. Although I was left with the impression that this was not the final fulfillment of Zechariah's prediction, God used it to make me realize just how close that fulfillment could be.

The Conflict Extended

In Zechariah 12:3, the prophet goes on to describe an extension of the conflict:

> "On that day, when all the nations of the earth are gathered against her, I will make Jerusalem an immovable rock for all the nations. All who try to move it will injure themselves."

In verse 2, the prophet spoke only of "all the surrounding peoples"—that is, the Arab states of the Middle East. To them, Jerusalem is "an intoxicating cup." Here in verse 3, Zechariah goes further by including "all the nations of the earth." To them, Jerusalem will be "an immovable rock," and any that attempt to move it will injure themselves.

In 1947–48, I watched the British mandatory government try to move this rock, but—just as Zechariah predicted—they injured themselves. Eventually they laid this "immovable rock" at the feet of the United Nations. Any other Gentile power that seeks to move this rock will suffer the same fate. Jerusalem is "the city of the Great King" (Matthew 5:35). The King alone can resolve the problems of His city and grant it true and lasting peace.

In light of the current world situation, it is not difficult to write a scenario climaxing with "all the nations of the earth gathered against Jerusalem." In fact, it takes no more than three scenes.

Scene 1: The Muslim bloc in the United Nations, with their allies, revives the proposal to make Jerusalem an international city. It is quite probable that the hierarchies of the Roman Catholic and Eastern Orthodox Churches—perhaps also the Anglican Church—would support this proposal.

Scene 2: The United Nations Assembly endorses the proposal and agrees to use military force, if necessary, to bring it about. Israel rejects the proposal.

Scene 3: The United Nations raises a representative military force, advances against Israel from one of the neighboring Arab territories and lays siege to Jerusalem. In this way, "all the nations of the earth" would, representatively, be "gathered against Jerusalem."

In the present state of world politics, the first "scene" outlined above could be enacted within a few days. Thereafter, it would take only a few weeks for the two subsequent "scenes" to become an accomplished historical fact. I am not necessarily suggesting that history will follow exactly the course I have outlined. My intention is merely to point out that we may already be at or near the threshold of the events predicted here by Zechariah.

The Bible's total picture of the close of the present age may be compared to a vast jigsaw puzzle. To make the complete picture, many pieces have to be assembled from a multitude of different prophetic passages. Many of the pieces from this passage in Zechariah are already on hand. There are probably pieces from other prophetic passages, however, which are required to complete the picture, that have yet to be assembled.

I question whether any human mind is capable, in advance, of putting together all the pieces in their correct places. In many cases, we can understand the full outworking of Bible prophecy only after it has actually taken place. Then, like Peter on the Day of Pentecost, we can say, "This is what was spoken by the prophet" (Acts 2:16).

At present, these prophecies of Zechariah—and many similar prophecies from various parts of the Bible—fulfill three important functions. First, they show us very clearly the general direction in which world events are moving. Second, they enable us to align ourselves with the outworking of God's predetermined purposes. Third, they warn us that the climax of the age could well be close at hand.

The Climax

For the final, dramatic climax of Zechariah's predictions concerning Israel and Jerusalem, we must turn to chapter 14:

I will gather all the nations to Jerusalem to fight against it; the city will be captured, the houses ransacked, and the women raped. Half of the city will go into exile, but the rest of the people will not be taken from the city.

Then the LORD will go out and fight against those nations, as he fights in the day of battle. On that day his feet will stand on the Mount of Olives, east of Jerusalem, and the Mount of Olives will be split in two from east to west, forming a great valley, with half of the mountain moving north and half moving south. . . . Then the LORD my God will come, and all the holy ones with him.

verses 2–5

In all probability, this passage depicts the final outcome of the gathering of all nations against Jerusalem, which was referred to first in Zechariah 12:3. It also seems reasonable to set these events in the period described by Jeremiah:

"How awful that day will be!
None will be like it.
It will be a time of trouble for Jacob,
but he will be saved out of it."

Jeremiah 30:7

It is not my purpose to examine all the details that are depicted so vividly here. Suffice it to say that the climax comes with the direct, personal intervention of the Lord Himself.

Anticipation of this glorious climax continues among God's people in the New Testament. In 2 Thessalonians, for example, Paul looks forward to this same event:

This will happen when the Lord Jesus is revealed from heaven in blazing fire with his powerful angels . . . on the day he comes to be glorified in his holy people and to be marveled at among all those who have believed.

2 Thessalonians 1:7, 10

In Revelation 22:13, Jesus declares Himself to be "the Alpha and the Omega" of all history. As the Alpha, He set history in motion.

Thereafter, other persons and agents have played their various parts. But when the end comes, it will again be Jesus who reappears as the Omega and brings history to its divinely ordained consummation.

In this consummation, the severed strands of history are reunited. The invisible becomes visible; the spiritual blends with the natural. Prophecy becomes history. The *written* Word of Scripture merges into the *personal* Word—the Lord made manifest. Their merging accomplishes the full and final outworking of *the last word on the Middle East.*

In this closing scene, all the actors in the drama of establishing God's Kingdom on earth are brought together on stage. It is the same stage on which every previous crisis of the same drama has been enacted: Jerusalem and the mountains that surround it. Angelic hosts, glorified saints and the preserved remnant of Israel take their respective places.

But the central figure, outshining all the rest and drawing them together around Himself, is that of Messiah, the King.

Thus heaven will vindicate the confession that every Orthodox Jew has maintained through the long centuries—even on his way to the stake or to the gas chamber: "I believe with perfect faith in the coming of the Messiah; and even if he tarries, still I will wait every day for him to come."

Thus, too, will heaven answer the prayer of the aged apostle John on the isle of Patmos—the prayer echoed by every true Christian as he closes his New Testament:

Amen. Come, Lord Jesus.

Special Section

Chronology of Events in Israel 1947–2004

November 29, 1947

Britain surrenders mandate over "Palestine." Vote of United Nations for the partitioning of the country into two independent states, Jewish and Arab. Arabs announce they will not accept a Jewish state but will take all of the country by force.

May 14, 1948

Declaration of Independence signed, a provisional government formed and the state of Israel proclaimed by David Ben Gurion. The Israel Defense Force (*Tzahal*) formed.

May 15, 1948

Surrounding Arab nations—Egypt, Transjordan, Syria, Lebanon, Iraq and Saudi Arabia—attack the new state.

May 17, 1948

U.S. under President Truman formally recognizes state of Israel.

January 7, 1949

Cease-fire ends War of Independence. (Armistice agreement signed July 1949; Arab League, however, closes its frontiers to Israel and declares itself "in a permanent state of war" with Israel.)

January 25, 1949

Israel holds first regular elections.

February 17, 1949

First *Knesset* (Parliament) meets in Jerusalem, elects Chaim Weizmann first president. He calls upon David Ben Gurion, first prime minister, to form first government. Provisional government resigns.

May 11, 1949

Israel admitted to United Nations.

1948–1951

Period of "Mass Immigration." Main aspects:

1. *Knesset* enacts Law of Return: "Every Jew has the right to come to this country as an immigrant."
2. Population more than doubles with 684,000 new arrivals: Holocaust survivors from Europe; refugees from Muslim countries of North Africa and the Middle East; airlift of entire Jewish communities from Yemen (43,000) and Iraq (113,000).
3. Diverse cultures and traditions of returning European (*Ashkenazi*) and Oriental (*Sephardi*) Jews.
4. Immediate problems for new nation: housing, food, employment.
5. Israel completes 78,000 dwellings; establishes 345 new villages in these 3 years (compared to 293 in previous 70 years).
6. Western Jews (particularly Americans) support financially, but few immigrate during this period.

1948–1956

Fedayeen (armed incursions) from neighboring countries, notably Egypt. Over 6,000 attacks with 1,300 Israelis killed.

1951

First World Zionist Congress meets in Jerusalem.

1952

West Germany signs reparations agreement to pay state of Israel $715 million and individuals $100 million for material losses to Jews under Nazism.

1955

Egypt forms military pact with Syria and Iraq, joined by Jordan. Egypt's President Nasser calls for destruction of state of Israel.

1956

Increase in terrorist attacks. Egypt blocks Straits of Tiran and effectively cuts off Israeli shipping routes.

October 1956

Suez crisis provokes the Sinai campaign. Israel attacks with support from France and Britain. Much equipment captured from Egyptians. Straits reopened. Cease-fire agreed on November 5.

1956–1962

Large-scale immigration from North Africa.

March 1957

Israel withdraws from Sinai. UN prevents further Egyptian infiltration until 1967.

1958

Major successes of the first decade of the state:

1. New immigrants assimilated—Hebrew widely taught and spoken.

2. Standard of living rising for Oriental (*Sephardi*) Jews; many becoming self-sufficient.

3. Agricultural self-sufficiency; 400 percent increase in irrigated areas; major reforestation.

4. Jewish population reaches 1.8 million; unemployment at 1.4 percent.

5. 150,000 new dwellings completed.

6. School population now at 550,000; universities enroll 10,000.

7. Increasing emphasis on Jewish cultural and spiritual heritage; e.g., World Bible Conference in Jerusalem sponsored by government.

8. Arab and Druse communities share in progress: 600 percent increase in their agricultural productivity; free universal primary education; national insurance; social welfare and health services; roads; water; electricity; sanitary facilities; irrigation. Participation in free elections; representation in *Knesset*.

1958–1959

Relations with emerging nations:

1. Israel gives technical and scientific assistance to emerging nations of Africa and Latin America, especially in the fields of agriculture and of upgrading living standards for undereducated and underprivileged people.

2. Many African and Latin American nations locate their embassies in Jerusalem and support Israel in the UN.

1964

Palestine Liberation Organization (PLO) established, calling for the destruction of the state of Israel.

1965–1966

Further progress in the following areas:

1. Exports of agricultural products total $86 million, chiefly citrus crops.

2. National water carrier completed, bringing water from upper Jordan River to Negev Desert in the south.

3. Burgeoning industry begins manufacturing hard goods (radios, refrigerators) for consumers. On the other hand, decreasing immigration—30,000 in 1965; 16,000 in 1966—brings slump in construction and related industries.

1967

Prelude to Six-Day War:

1. *Al Fatah*, Palestinian terrorist organization, sending trained terrorists into Israel for sabotage.

2. Syrians bombarding *kibbutz* settlements in Galilee.

3. May 14: Nasser moves large numbers of Egyptian troops into Sinai.

4. May 16: Nasser expels UN peacekeeping force from Sinai.

5. May 24: Nasser blocks Strait of Tiran at entrance to Gulf of Aqaba (and Port of Eilat).

6. May 26: Nasser announces that Egypt is "prepared to wage war on Israel."

7. May 30: King Hussein places Jordan's military forces under Nasser's control.

8. June 4: Iraq follows suit. Israel mobilizes for defense. Older men, women and children keep services going, bring in the harvest, pack export orders.

1967

Six-Day War:

June 5

1. Israel bombs airfields of Egypt, Syria, Jordan and Iraq, destroying 452 planes in 3 hours.

2. Israeli ground forces move against Egyptian forces in the Sinai at four points.

3. Israel notifies King Hussein that it will not attack Jordan if his troops keep the peace. Jordanian troops, however, open fire

along entire armistice line and occupy UN headquarters in Jerusalem.

June 6

Israel counterattacks and takes all of Jerusalem except Old City.

June 7

Israel gains possession of Old City of Jerusalem for the first time since AD 70.

June 9

Israel drives Syrians from the heavily fortified Golan Heights. Israel penetrates Sinai to Suez Canal; takes Gaza Strip; naval forces capture Sharm-el-Sheikh on the Red Sea.

June 10

All parties agree to cease-fire. In various ways, the Six-Day War was marked by the same kind of miraculous elements as the War of Independence.

Jerusalem declared the "Eternal Capital of the State of Israel."

June 1967

Israel establishes the following policy for occupied Arab territories:

1. Guarantees free access to holy places of all three faiths.
2. Takes down barriers between East and West Jerusalem.
3. Institutes "Open Bridges" policy, which is accepted by Jordan's King Hussein. Arabs living in Judea, Samaria (the "West Bank") and Gaza Strip are thus able to travel freely to Arab countries, sell their produce in Jordan and receive visits of relatives and friends. Tourists also are free to enter Israel through Jordan.
4. Announces it will accept applications to return from the 200,000 Arabs who fled during the fighting (44,000 have returned).

1967–1968

Unprecedented awakening of Jews abroad to Israel's importance for world Jewry. Large influx of immigrants from the West, especially young people. Financial contributions from the Diaspora total $400 million in these two years. Beginning of aliyah from USSR, contested by Soviet authorities, and incarceration of "refuseniks" in Russian jails.

1968–1973

"War of Attrition":

1. Continual harassment by Egypt on Sinai borders.
2. Increasing Soviet involvement in Egypt: Soviet pilots in Soviet planes, antiaircraft missile bases manned by Soviet crews.
3. Syrians also receive Soviet assistance; regularly shell Israel's northern border with Soviet *katyusha* rockets.
4. Palestinian terrorist activity increasing from north through Lebanon border. (King Hussein had bombed Palestinian terrorist camps and driven terrorists out of Jordan in 1970; they resettled in southern Lebanon, which became known as "Fatahland.")
5. Increasing Arab terrorism outside Israel: airplane hijackings, murder of Israeli athletes at Munich Olympics in 1971.

1970

Palestinians driven from Jordan to Lebanon.

1973

Prelude to *Yom Kippur* War:

October 5

1. Egyptian and Syrian troops massing on cease-fire lines.
2. Israel begins mobilization of reserves on eve of *Yom Kippur* (Day of Atonement).
3. Prime Minister Golda Meir, notified of "unmistakable signs of imminent attack," rules against preemptive air strike "to make the responsibility for aggression unmistakably clear."

October 6

Yom Kippur War:

1. Israeli cabinet meets on the holy day itself, confirms Golda Meir's decision.

2. On Israel's national day of mourning, Arabs attack on two fronts at 2 p.m. as Israeli cabinet is meeting.

   a. In the south: Egyptian aircraft and artillery bombard installations in Sinai; seventy thousand troops and one thousand tanks cross Suez Canal.

   b. In the north: forty thousand Syrian troops with eight hundred tanks attack on Golan Heights.

October 7–25

3. Israel stops advance on both fronts within two days, but at heavy cost; Soviet antiaircraft and antitank weapons batter Israeli planes and tanks.

4. Iraq joins Syria in the war.

5. After Soviets began airlift of the equipment to Egypt and Syria on October 10, U.S. begins airlift of ammunition and spare parts to Israel on October 14.

6. Israel penetrates 12–15 miles beyond cease-fire lines on Syrian front (within 25 miles of Damascus).

7. Israeli army crosses into Egypt on October 16 and raids missile bases and military installations behind Egyptian army lines; advances within 62 miles of Cairo.

8. As Arab nations face defeat, Soviets join U.S. in call for cease-fire; accepted on October 23.

9. Egyptians and Syrians continue firing; Israelis wait twelve hours, then counterattack.

10. October 25: Soviet military on alert, ready to intervene in Egypt; U.S. armed forces placed on worldwide alert.

11. October 25: Cease-fire holds. For first time in Arab-Israeli history, a cease-fire agreement contains provision for direct peace negotiations.

October–November 1973

After the cease-fire—beginning of the "Oil War":

1. OPEC (Organization of Petroleum Exporting Countries), which had announced reduction of oil production by 5 percent until Israel withdrew from all territories, now cuts off oil supplies to the U.S. and Holland.

2. After OPEC reduced oil supplies by 25 percent to common market states and Japan, these countries issue statements favoring Arab cause.

3. Most black African states break diplomatic relations with Israel because of dependence on Arab oil and in interests of African solidarity.

4. November 28: Arab summit conference calls for intensifying oil pressure against Israel.

5. OPEC raises oil prices from $2.59 per barrel in January 1973 to $11.65 per barrel in December. (Oil costs for Third World nations increased from $12 billion in 1973 to $30 billion in 1974 to $42 billion in 1975.)

1973–1979

Arab terrorists infiltrate Israel, plant explosives, kill civilians. Led by Yasser Arafat's *Al Fatah*, they are joined by other groups. Known collectively as the PLO, they are financed by Arab oil-producing nations. Between 1973 and 1979, there were 1,575 terrorist attacks within Israel; e.g.:

1974

Ma'alot: Sixteen schoolchildren on outing slaughtered by terrorists.

1975

Zion Square, Jerusalem: Bomb kills 15 passersby, wounds 62.

1978

Tel Aviv highway: Busload of hikers exploded with incendiary bomb; 34 killed, including women and children.

While Israel is the primary target of the PLO, airports, airlines and embassies in any country deemed friendly to Israel are subject to PLO attack. Between 1967 and 1978, outside of Israel, Arab terrorists killed 1,133 people, wounded 2,498 and held 2,755 hostage. These included a Swiss-Air jet that blew up in midair in February 1970, killing 47; a machine-gun attack on French passengers in Orly Airport, Paris, in May 1978.[12]

January 18, 1974

Egypt and Israel sign disengagement agreement; hailed by U.S. as first step toward permanent Middle East peace.

May 1974

Syria and Israel sign disengagement agreement. Israel withdraws slightly west of 1967 cease-fire lines on Golan Heights.

September 1975

Israel withdraws from portions of Sinai; Egypt reopens Suez Canal to Israeli shipping for first time since 1951.

January 1976

Syria intervenes on side of PLO in Lebanese civil war. Southern Lebanon used as base for extensive *katyusha* rocket attacks on Israeli settlements.

July 1976

Israeli forces, in daring rescue operation, release 103 hostages held by Arab terrorists in a hijacked plane at Entebbe Airport in Uganda and bring them home to Israel.

July 1977

Prime Minister Menachem Begin presents plan for Middle East peace to President Carter in Washington.

November 1977

Egyptian President Anwar Sadat visits Jerusalem at invitation of Prime Minister Begin to address *Knesset*.

September 1978

Prime Minister Begin, President Sadat and President Carter meet at Camp David, Maryland; formulate peace accords.

March 26, 1979

Israel and Egypt sign peace treaty. They agree to recognize and respect each other's right to live in peace within secure and recognized borders and to establish regular diplomatic relations.

Israel further agrees:

1. To withdraw to line of former mandate border with Egypt.
2. To hand over intact to Egypt the Alma oilfields that Israel had located and developed.
3. To redeploy Israel defense forces located in the Sinai, and to transfer to Egypt intact roads, utilities, water supply points and other installations, including three major airfields. (Egypt agrees to use these for civilian purposes only.)

Egypt further agrees:

1. To permit Israeli shipping through the Suez Canal.
2. To sell oil to Israel at market price.

1979

In response to increasing civilian casualties, Israel begins preemptive strikes against terrorist bases in southern Lebanon. Israel also trains and assists Lebanese Christian army under command of Major Saad Haddad.

1979–82

Escalating conflict in southern Lebanon in response to extensive attacks on Israel.

1980

Knesset declares all of united Jerusalem to be the capital of Israel.

1981

North of Israel under daily bombardment by PLO/Syrian forces; residents, including children, spend weeks in shelters. (Some children evacuated to safe areas.) Villages, orchards, farm equipment and crops destroyed. Israel retaliates by bombing PLO headquarters in Beirut. In July, a cease-fire is negotiated. The current situation remains unstable and explosive.

June 7, 1981

In a lightning attack, Israeli fighters bomb and destroy the nearly completed Osiraq nuclear reactor near Baghdad, Iraq. Strong evidence indicated it was to be used to develop nuclear weapons capability for Saddam Hussein.

December 14, 1981

Israel annexes the Golan Heights.

April 25, 1982

Israel officially returns the Sinai to Egypt in a special ceremony, having completed the three-step withdrawal negotiated at Camp David.

June 1982

Israel invades Lebanon in Operation Peace for Galilee. PLO forced to leave Beirut for Tunis; 650 Israelis killed in conflict. Palestinian terrorists attempt to assassinate Israel's ambassador to Great Britain, Shlomo Argov, severely wounding him. Killings at Sabra and Shatila refugee camps by Lebanese Christian Phalangist militia cause a furor in Israel, leading to the dismissal of Defense Minister Ariel Sharon and Army Chief of Staff Gen. Raful Eitan.

1983

Hyperinflation in Israel reaches a peak of 445 percent. Menachem Begin resigns as prime minister.

1984

After mid-year elections, a first-ever Labor-Likud coalition government is formed, with Shimon Peres of Labor installed as prime minister.

November 18, 1984

Operation Moses repatriates nearly eight thousand Ethiopian Jews to Israel in just six weeks.

April 22, 1985

Establishment of a free trade agreement between Israel and the U.S.

June–July 1985

Israeli withdrawal from Lebanon except for forty-mile security zone in southern Lebanon.

1986

Inflation brought down to 19.7 percent.

October 13, 1986

As part of the coalition agreement negotiated in 1984, Yitzhak Shamir of Likud takes over as prime minister.

December 10, 1987

First Palestinian *Intifada* ("throwing off"). Allegedly a "popular uprising," involving strikes, demonstrations, riots and violence, in protest of Israeli "occupation" of Gaza and the West Bank. Symbolized by media coverage of Palestinian men and boys throwing stones at Israeli defense forces and civilians.

1989

Start of massive immigration by Soviet Jews. (Between 1989 and 2002, approximately eight hundred thousand Soviet Jews returned to Israel—this, in a nation whose total population is only 6 million. Their absorption strained the resources of the Jewish state to the breaking point, yet somehow they were effectively integrated into the fabric of Israeli society. Such a phenomenon has no parallel in the history of modern human migrations.)

1990

Iraq invades neighboring Kuwait. U.S. builds a coalition of forces, under UN agreement, to force Iraq out of Kuwait and protect Western interests in the Persian Gulf area.

January–February 1991

In January, the Gulf War begins. Iraq responds by launching 39 Scud missiles into Israeli population centers, though Israel is not directly involved in the war. There is much loss of property, but in a modern-day miracle, only two are killed as a direct result of the missiles.

Iraq defeated by American-led coalition. Israel agrees to be noncombatant to maintain Arab support for coalition.

May 30, 1991

Operation Solomon: In an unprecedented rescue operation, 14,324 Ethiopian Jews (nearly the entire remaining Jewish population of Ethiopia) are airlifted and resettled in Israel in less than two days.

1992

Diplomatic relations are established with India and China.

A new government is formed, headed by Labor's Yitzhak Rabin.

August–September 1993

After secret negotiations near Oslo, Norway, a peace initiative, the Oslo Declaration of Principles, is proposed by Israel. The proposal introduces the concept of "peace for land," including establishment of Palestinian self-rule by 1999, in return for a cessation of the *Intifada*, peace with neighboring Arab states and gradual assumption of governmental responsibilities for the disputed territories by the Palestinian Authority. Israel offers to be a partner in an international resolution to the Arab refugee problem. Documents formalizing the proposal are signed in Washington, D.C., by Yitzhak Rabin and Yasser Arafat, signaling Israel's recognition and acceptance of the PLO as the official representative of the Palestinian people.

1994

Substantial increase in violence against civilians. An Israeli settler kills 29 Palestinians in a mosque in Hebron. A Hamas suicide bomber blows up a bus in Tel Aviv, killing 22 and injuring 47.

August 29, 1994

Agreement is reached whereby Jericho and most of the Gaza Strip is transferred to PLO control.

October 26, 1994

Peace treaty signed between Israel and the Hashemite kingdom of Jordan.

December 10, 1994

Shimon Peres, Yitzhak Rabin and Yasser Arafat are awarded the Nobel Peace Prize.

1995

On September 28, the Oslo Interim Agreement on the West Bank and Gaza Strip is signed. A further Israeli withdrawal from Judea and Samaria is carried out. This transfer of land allows 97 percent of Palestinians outside of Jerusalem to govern their own lives.

Despite this agreement, widespread and unprecedented Palestinian terrorist attacks take a heavy toll. More Israelis are killed by terror attacks during the 5 years after the Oslo Accords (278 killed) than in the preceding 15 years (254 killed).

November 4, 1995

Shortly after giving a speech at a Tel Aviv peace rally, Prime Minister Yitzhak Rabin is assassinated by Jewish right-wing extremist Yigal Amir, who was opposed to a peace treaty with the Palestinians. Shimon Peres is sworn in as prime minister.

1996

Israel establishes trade representation offices in Qatar and Oman.

March 1996

Operation Grapes of Wrath launched against Hezbollah in southern Lebanon.

May 29, 1996

Promising to deal more effectively with the Palestinian violence, Benjamin Netanyahu is chosen in the first direct elections for prime minister of Israel. In August, he lifts the ban imposed in 1992 on the establishment of new Jewish settlements in the West Bank, increasing by nearly 50,000 residents the Jewish presence in "occupied" territories.

1997

On January 17, an agreement of redeployment from Hebron is signed, and most of the city is turned over by Israel to the Palestinian Authority (the PA).

May 14, 1998

Israel celebrates its fiftieth anniversary!

October 23, 1998

Wye River Memorandum is signed by Yasser Arafat and Benjamin Netanyahu, outlining the implementation of the "Interim Agreement on the West Bank and Gaza Strip" signed in September 1995. This gives the Palestinians another 13 percent of Israeli-controlled land in the West Bank. The ailing King Hussein of Jordan and U.S. President William Clinton attend the ceremony.

1999

Ehud Barak is elected prime minister on a platform of peace.

May 2000

Israeli and Christian militia withdraw from southern Lebanon, abandoning its "security zone," thus fulfilling UN resolution 425. Despite this withdrawal, terrorist attacks at the border continue, as well as attempted infiltrations.

July–August 2000

Arafat rejects an offer of 94 percent of the disputed territories, including a portion of East Jerusalem. Included in the offer was permission for tens of thousands of Palestinian expatriates to return and be reunited with their families.

September 2000

On September 13, the seventh anniversary of the Oslo Declaration of Principles, the Palestinians respond to the Israeli offer by releasing convicted terrorists, attacking Israeli settlements and army outposts and patrols, and inflicting more car bombings and suicide attacks.

December 9, 2000

Prime Minister Barak resigns in frustration amid the intensifying violence.

January–February 2001

The Palestinian Authority is offered nearly 100 percent of the territories in question, again including East Jerusalem and an agreement for repatriation of Palestinian exiles. Again the offer is rejected, resulting in even more violence by Palestinian extremists.

February 2001

Ariel Sharon is elected prime minister. He names Shimon Peres, leader of the main opposition party and an architect of the Oslo Accords, as foreign minister in a national unity government.

September 11, 2001

Al Qaeda Islamic extremists, with links to the Palestinian groups Hezbollah and Hamas, destroy the twin towers of the World Trade Center in New York and damage the Pentagon, killing nearly three thousand people in suicide airplane attacks. In Gaza and the West Bank, Palestinians dance in the streets, chanting their support for the leader of Al Qaeda, Osama bin Laden.

January 3, 2002

The *Karine A*, a ship owned by the Palestinian Authority and headed to the port of Gaza, is intercepted by the Israeli Navy and Defense Forces and found to be loaded with weapons purchased from the Iranian government by a top Arafat lieutenant.

March 29, 2002

The Israeli Defense Forces launch Operation Defensive Shield, reoccupying much of the territories previously turned over to the PA. In the process, they trap Arafat in his headquarters in Ramallah and uncover considerable evidence indicating his active complicity in the suicide bombings and other attacks upon Israeli citizens and forces. Amid repeatedly disproven accusations of violence against Palestinian civilians, the IDF enters refugee camps at Jenin, Nablus and elsewhere, attempting to destroy the ability of the terrorist cells of Hamas, Fatah and Hezbollah to wage war on Israel.

May 2002

Arafat, weakened by revelations from within the PA that he has stolen more than $1 billion from PA coffers and hidden it in Swiss accounts, and under growing pressure for democratic reforms, signs into law the Basic Law, or constitution of the Palestinian transitional state. It says that Palestinian law will be based upon the principles of Sharia (Islamic law).

June 2002

U.S. President George W. Bush calls for the Palestinian people to "elect new leaders . . . not compromised by terror [and] . . . official corruption." At the same time, he urges Israel to work toward "two states, living side by side in peace and security."

October 2002

The Labor party withdraws from the Israel unity government. Prime Minister Ariel Sharon calls for elections to be held in January, and the Likud party wins a strong mandate to continue hard-line policies against the Palestinians.

2003

After 1977, expansion of the settlements became official Israeli government policy. By 2003, approximately 225,000 Israelis had established themselves in the West Bank and Gaza. At least 200,000 more were settled in the areas of Jerusalem conquered in 1967. An estimated 20,000 settlers had moved into the portions of the Golan captured from Syria.

March 20, 2003

U.S., British and Australian forces invade Iraq. Most Palestinians support Saddam Hussein, who had provided payments of $25,000 to families of suicide bombers. On April 9, U.S. forces enter Baghdad, and on May 1, primary ground operations are declared completed. The swiftness of Iraq's collapse astounds the Middle East. Arab governments, including the Palestinian Authority, Syria and Libya, hurriedly make conciliatory gestures toward the U.S.

April 29, 2003

Mahmud Abbas, also known as Abu Mazen, is elected Palestinian prime minister, with the approval of Arafat, but the violence continues.

June 4, 2003

Israeli Prime Minister Sharon and new Palestinian Prime Minister Abbas pledge to fulfill the conditions of the redesigned "Road Map for Peace," shaking hands in the presence of U.S. President George W. Bush.

September 2003

Abbas resigns after his attempts to arrest several known Palestinian terror leaders are thwarted by Arafat. He is replaced by Palestinian hard-liner Ahmed Qureia.

The security fence, originally a Labor party idea that contributed to their defeat in the January 2003 elections, is adopted and adapted by Prime Minister Ariel Sharon. He redesigns the route of the fence to include several previously excluded settlements. The intent is to make terror attacks on Israeli soil nearly impossible. A similar fence erected previously in a part of Gaza had successfully reduced suicide infiltrations from that location to zero.

End of 2003

Prime Minister Ariel Sharon surprises everyone by announcing a unilateral plan to withdraw all IDF forces and settlers from the Gaza Strip and from several parts of the West Bank. His proposal is met by angry resistance from his Cabinet, his own Likud party members and affected settlers.

March 2004

While Hamas members had been "targets of opportunity" for the IDF for several years, 2003 and 2004 saw a marked escalation in attacks on their local and national leaders. On March 22, 2004, Sheikh Ahmed Yassin, the spiritual leader of Hamas, is killed in a rocket attack. Though blind and wheelchair bound, he had been responsible for the deaths of hundreds of people and had repeatedly sabotaged the peace process.

His replacement, Dr. Abdel Aziz Rantissi, is eliminated by Israeli forces on April 17, leaving Dr. Mahmoud Zahar as the last of the seven founders of Hamas still living. No official announcement is made as to who will assume the reins of Hamas.

April 2004

Israeli Prime Minister Ariel Sharon travels to the U.S. to garner American support for his disengagement plan. President Bush publicly states his acceptance of the plan and declares that the "Road Map for Peace" remains the only peace plan backed by the United States. Additionally, to help the beleaguered Sharon back in Israel, Bush advances that Palestinian refugees should be repatriated to the new Palestinian state, rather than Israel. President Bush also adds that Israel should not have to withdraw to the 1949 borders and that the U.S. will not oppose the construction of the Israeli security fence.

This announcement meets with universal opposition from the Arab world, the UN and most world leaders.

As this book goes to press, there is enormous pressure upon Israel, from friend and foe alike, to "divide the land" in exchange for peace.

Economic and Military Pressures

The constant need for sophisticated weaponry against surrounding Arab nations in a country with few valuable natural resources has created unparalleled pressures upon the tiny nation of Israel. The chart below portrays vividly the multiplicities of land, peoples, armies and weapons arrayed against Israel as of 2000:

The Arab World versus Israel

	Land Area (sq. mi.)	Population	Armed Forces	Combat Aircraft	Tanks
Israel	8,442	6,100,000	186,500 (445,000 reserves)	800	3,930
Arab League	5,109,230	218,007,000	698,930 (1,212,500 reserves)	10,875	1,641
Egypt	400,580	69,080,000	450,000 (254,000 reserves)	494	3,505

(The Arab League in this table consists of Jordan, Iraq, Iran, Syria and Saudi Arabia. Egypt is listed separately because of their peace treaty with Israel.)

(Excerpted from Tigay and Feldman)

The following chart demonstrates the financial sacrifice Israel has made for peace with Egypt:

The Cost of Peace

Sinai: Airfields, bases and facilities	$10 billion
Oilfields*	5 billion
Roads and settlements	2 billion
Subtotal:	$17 billion**
Redeployment of Israel defense forces from Sinai to Negev	4.4 billion
Total:	$21.4 billion

* These fields provided 20 percent of Israel's annual need.

** This figure almost equals Israel's foreign debt for 1980, $18 billion.

(Reprinted from *North Broward Jewish Chronicle*, Jan. 9, 1981)

The preceding chart does not include the cost of remuneration for Israelis who had settled in and developed the Sinai, which is in excess of $500 million.

The boycott against Israel by the Arab oil-producing nations has caused an additional economic burden for Israel: They pay the highest prices for oil on the world market. In 1980, this amounted to $2.4 billion, which equaled almost exactly their balance of payments deficit.

These two related problems—the cost of defense and the cost of oil—created a related problem: mounting inflation. The following chart indicates the instability of the Israeli lira (pound)*, which is designated IL and compared here with the American dollar.

Comparative Value of Currency

1948	IL	0.20	$1.00 (approx.)
1962	IL	3.00	$1.00
1973	IL	4.20	$1.00
1978	IL	15.00	$1.00
1982	IL	160.00 (ILS 16.00)*	$1.00
1995	ILS	3.02	$1.00
2002	ILS	4.92	$1.00
2004	ILS	4.89	$1.00

* In 1980, Israel adopted new currency, the *shekel* (ILS – Israel Shekel), which equals IL 10. In 1973, the Israeli lira was worth a little less than 25 cents (U.S.). In 1982, the equivalent of one Israeli lira is worth a little less than 3/4 cent (U.S.). By 1983, inflation reached an incredible 445 percent! However, severe budget cuts (causing a severe recession) managed to bring inflation down to 19.7 percent by 1984. By the year 2000, inflation was brought to 0. Given the almost impossible task of absorbing almost 1 million immigrants from 1990 to 2000 and the huge expenses involved, as well as the tremendous defense burden, this was a modern-day miracle (see Ezekiel 36:34–35). By 2002, the per capita GDP had risen to $19,700 but was still less than Canada, Spain or New Zealand.

Some Statistics of Israel at Age 52

	1960s	1970s	1980s	2000
Population (hundred thousands)	2,150	3,022	3,922	6,203
Jews in Israel (percent of total world Jewry)	13%	20%	25%	37%
Gross Domestic Product (billions)	$2.5	$6.8	$19.1	$100
Exports (millions)	$217	$768	$5,511	$23,285
Tourists	110,000	419,000	1,066,000	2,010,000
Private Cars	24,000	148,000	410,000	1,273,000
Telephone Subscribers	68,000	369,000	860,000	2,804,000

Statistics from The Jewish Student Online Research Center (JSource) May 2000, based on figures from the Statistical Abstract of Israel, No. 50, 1999.

NOTES

1. Edward H. Flannery, *The Anguish of the Jews* (New York: Macmillan Publishing Co., Inc., 1965), 60.

2. Solomon Grayzel, *A History of the Jews* (Philadelphia: The Jewish Publications Society of America, 1947), 464.

3. Ibid., 465.

4. Franz Kobler, *The Vision Was There* (London: Lincolns-Prager Ltd., 1956), 24.

5. Ibid., 42.

6. Claude Duvernoy, *The Prince and the Prophet* (Jerusalem: Claude Duvernoy, 1979), 58.

7. Ibid., 115.

8. Flannery, *The Anguish of the Jews*, 48.

9. Ibid., 49.

10. Marius Baar, *The Unholy War* (Nashville: Thomas Nelson Publishers, 1980), 121.

11. Reprinted from *Toronto Daily Star*, May 15, 1965.

12. Alan M. Tigay, ed., *Myths and Facts 1980. A Concise Record of the Arab-Israeli Conflict* (Washington, D.C.: Near East Research, Inc., 1980), 122–23.

INDEX

Derek Prince (1915–2003) was born in India of British parents. Educated as a scholar of Greek and Latin at Eton College and Cambridge University, England, he held a fellowship in ancient and modern philosophy at King's College. He also studied several modern languages, including Hebrew and Aramaic, at Cambridge University and the Hebrew University in Jerusalem.

While serving with the British army in World War II, he began to study the Bible and experienced a life-changing encounter with Jesus Christ. Out of this encounter he formed two conclusions: first, that Jesus Christ is alive; second, that the Bible is a true, relevant, up-to-date book. These conclusions altered the whole course of his life, which he then devoted to studying and teaching the Bible.

Derek's main gift of explaining the Bible and its teaching in a clear and simple way has helped build a foundation of faith in millions of lives. His nondenominational, nonsectarian approach has made his teaching equally relevant and helpful to people from all racial and religious backgrounds.

He is the author of over fifty books and five hundred audio and one hundred sixty video teaching cassettes, many of which have been translated and published in more than sixty languages. His daily radio broadcast, *Keys to Successful Living*, is translated into Arabic, Chinese (Amoy, Cantonese, Mandarin, Shanghaiese, Swatow), Croatian, German, Malagasy, Mongolian, Russian, Samoan, Spanish and Tongan. His daily radio program continues to touch lives around the world.

For more information, please call or write:

Derek Prince Ministries
P.O. Box 19501
Charlotte, NC 28219-9501
USA
(704) 357-3556
www.dpmusa.org